Flow Blue China
An Aid to Identification

REVISED EDITION

THE STUDIO
FOUNTAIN HOUSE EAST

Petra Williams

Flow Blue China

An Aid to Identification

REVISED EDITION

FOUNTAIN HOUSE EAST

Jeffersontown, Kentucky

Dedicated

to

Marguerite Rose Weber

Without whose help this book would not

have been completed.

FOREWORD

In each of us lies buried the genesis of a book. Each life is different. We are bound together in mortality, but like snowflakes, each of us is unique. Our dreams, motives and interests differ, too. Necessity sets us on paths we do not expect, and so does curiosity. I never would have dreamed that I would be obsessed to write a monograph about Flow Blue China.

Like so many other women, I hold on to my share of my ancestors' effects, cherishing them for the memories that they evoke, and hoping to pass them on unscathed to my children. In this trove of my heritage are some simple blue and white printed dishes. At an auction in Louisville, Kentucky, some china like mine was put up for bidding and I became infected with the collector's itch.

Trying to find out more about the wares and where they were made, and when, and what would be a fair value to pay for each item, I ran into a blank wall. Neither collectors nor dealers know much about these simple dishes.

Library reference works offered almost no help. It is possible to find definitions and that is about all. I had begun to buy and sell Flow Blue China in fairly large quantities when I finally decided to establish a small museum collection of pattern plates, because I realized that almost no one knows what she is doing when she buys in this field.

Historical Staffordshire has been well documented in this country by Laidecker, Larson and Little. Old china has been magnificently outlined by Kamm. The great patterns of the world have been written about by English writers like Godden and Cushion, but no one heretofore has tackled Flow Blue.

I gather that it has been considered a lowly subject. Connoisseurs prefer porcelains, China Trade, and the Historical ware made before 1835. Transfer ware was inexpensive to make and was sold fairly cheap. People of wealth may have bought a set to be used for second best, but if a family was middle class and wanted dishes that were durable and pretty, Flow Blue did very well. The variety of the patterns, those hundreds of designs fashioned from the same blue and white, are astonishing for their individuality.

Now, of course, a lot of Flow Blue is well over a century old and it is becoming rare. The attrition of constant use has taken its toll. It is difficult to acquire a service of the pattern of the 1860s and 1870s and almost impossible to acquire a service dating from 1840-1850 unless you are rich; then it's not easy. To judge by the doleful letters I have received, it is expensive to try to put together a complete set of the later Victorian periods.

Collecting is made more difficult by the confusing duplication of titles. I feel that if a collector can see the patterns in a book and learn how to identify marks, he or she can collect more easily, can combine patterns to form a set, and can buy, sell and trade with confidence. Therefore, this book of patterns.

I approach this writing most humbly. My education was for the law, but my life took a turn and I became an interior designer. I knew very little about antique china and had only a superficial knowledge about the dishes I treasured.

The knowledge of the various dealers in the trade never ceases to amaze me. They know a lot about a multiplicity of things and their scope of information, hard

i

learned, but freely and graciously given, always is a delight. When I read with awe the great chroniclers of antique pottery and porcelain, I can only wonder at their research and erudition.

For the purpose of this book we will start with patterns of the period of about 1835-1840, when Flow Blue first appeared on historical china, and we will stop at about 1910.

I would like to stop at 1900 but some collectable pottery was made after that and I receive many inquiries about Flow Blue after 1900.

Duplicate names of patterns are commonplace. Even if a pattern was registered, no one was prevented from using the same name for a different pattern. Duplication also occurred when a factory went bankrupt and was sold; the buyer would use the same name and pattern but would add his own factory mark.

Some of these patterns have become scarce collector's items and are highly prized in the market. Others, bearing the same name, may be of a later date, or they may be a little known pattern, so they are much lower priced. Not that price will always tell you which ones you are buying; there are still bargains to be found. But it can be an unsettling experience to purchase an "Argyle" sugar bowl, when you want "Grindley", with its heavily printed floral plumes and gold, and you unpack an Argyle piece which is Art Nouveau.

This is an incomplete list of duplicate names I am sure, but let it serve to point out, that when you order sight unseen, be certain to specify your pattern name, how the name is spelled, and the name of the manufacturer.

Albany	Geneva	Osborne
Arcadia	Holland	Poppy
Argyle	India	Richmond
Cambridge	Iris	Savoy
Celtic	Lahore	Scinde
Chinese	Madras	Shell
Duchess	Messina	Sterling
Excelsior	Nankin	Trent
Florida	Oregon	Verona
Formosa	Oriental	Watteau

The name Wedgwood on a piece of china may deceive you. Josiah Wedgwood of Etruria was the greatest Wedgwood of whom you read in histories of the Staffordshire potteries. Podmore Walker and Co. of Tunstall turned out a good deal of Flow Blue. Enoch Wedgwood was a partner in this firm. They usually marked their goods "Pearl Stone Ware", and "Wedgwood". You may find identical plates, one marked "PW&CO" and the other "Wedgwood". James Wood of Burslem employed the middle name of Wedg. He marked his goods "J. Wedg.wood". Sometimes he used a period in the space between Wedg and wood, sometimes he did not. But you will not find the letter "J" used on true Wedgwood. Another firm, William Smith and Co. used the mark W. S. & Co.'s Wedgwood/ware. A legal action by Wedgwood stopped this in 1848. Another firm (unknown) used "Vedgwood".

The colors on Flow Blue are not always cobalt, the rich, soft, dark, dark blue that is associated with the early historical ware. Cobalt was expensive, and other pigments were experimented with. The resulting blues were sometimes lighter, sometimes blacker, and often a slate color. But they were flown in the kiln by the process of instilling lime or chloride of ammonia, and many collectors prefer the greyer blues. The only criterion should be whether the blue was really intended to flow and whether the ware shows a blurring or bleeding. But this can fool you; I have seen very old patterns that are very blurred, and occasionally a piece of the same age and pattern will turn up that is as clear as it can be. The blue did not flow through the body of the china. Because you can see blue blurs on the bottom of a plate, does not mean that it came through the dish from the transfer pattern. It was deposited there during the instilling process and probably came from the plates below in the sagger. Some plates are very flown on the face and are without a tinge of blue on the reverse. These probably were at the bottom of the sagger. To prove this to yourself look at a broken piece of the ware, you will see that the body, even on very porous earthenware, is not dyed blue.

The photographs in this book are not of professional quality. Many were donated by collectors and dealers, and I am aware that they are not perfect. But if you will read the description and look at the picture, I am certain that in almost every case you can learn to identify the pattern.

There are mistakes in this book, I am sure. This may occur in dating pieces and their marks, but most have been placed in the correct time period. It has proved impossible to secure examples or photographs of all the names garnered, or seen listed at sale. If my readers know of other patterns that I have not found, perhaps they will correspond with me at Jeffersontown, Kentucky.

As far as prices are concerned it has been my experience that the rarer pieces of a set are much higher priced than those that were not used so often. Ten-inch dinner plates at today's prices cost from $12 to $30, depending on the pattern. Tea pots are from $45 to $135. Cups and saucers are selling from $15 to $30 according to pattern demand. Note that mismatched cups and saucers are being sold at antique shows. A rule of thumb as of this writing is six-inch plate $6, eight-inch plate $8, nine-inch plate $9, platters from $25 to $35, vegetable bowls, round or oval, $12 to $35. Covered tureens are selling from $35 to $50. A very large soup tureen with ladle and tray will go for about $100. Pitcher and bowl sets start at $60 to $75 and go to $150 to $175. Price is a matter of supply and demand, of course, but your Flow Blue will not depreciate in value, it can only grow older and more valuable.

There is some Flow Blue being made in Sweden now. The pattern is of very large grape leaves and small grapes. They are clearly backstamped "Vinranka" made by "Upsala-Ekeby Sweden Cefle." The cups are very large, like a farmers cup. (You can study this pattern in the Miscellaneous section of this book.) I have been told of factories that are busy putting out black market Flow Ware in this country, and that they are making reproductions, but so far I have been unable to trace these rumors. I doubt that many people would commit fraud and risk jail in order to sell dishes.

If you know your patterns and your marks while you are collecting, you will acquire a sense about an old dish or cup. The scratches on it, wear marks, stains, knife cuts, the very feel and weight, will help you to determine its value to you.

Some patterns that were advertised and sold to me as Flow Blue turned out to be nothing of the sort. If this happens to you, it will be because you did not ascertain pattern and mark and know what you were ordering . We were collecting for the purpose of photographs for this book and were sold the following which are not Flow Blue: Silverdale, Chatsworth, Togo (in pale blue) (this was made in flow cobalt), Ridgway's Oriental (in pale blue), Alhambra, Ferrara, and even Countryside that was used as a leader by the Kroger grocery chain in 1968, the latter were marked "pattern" No. 547269, which looked to read 1908, but this only meant that the pattern had been registered then, not that the plate was made at that time.

My grateful thanks to those friends, dealers and collectors who helped me so much, especially Edith T. Miller of Pennsylvania, Gail Dickerson from Connecticut, Maxine Smith, Elizabeth Lanham, Elizabeth Coke, Loren A. Smith, Valerie Williams, Olin King, M. Charmoli, G. Phillips, S. Surowski, Mrs. Edwin Dominique, the Burgomaster of Masstricht, Holland, and Mr. Frank Van der Berge of Amsterdam, Mr. Henry Cushion, The William Adams Co., Ltd., Doulton, & Co., Ltd., the Museum at Staffordshire, and F. V. Woolsey of Louisville, who was kind enough to edit my manuscript.

Finally, in describing the patterns I have decided not to editorialize. That is, I will not write that a pattern is beautiful, or that it is not. Beauty is in the eye of the collector and to each his own preference. I hope simply to give you some help in seeking out and identifying the pieces of Flow Blue for which you are searching — and good luck!

Jeffersontown, Ky. June, 1971

Petra Williams

FOREWORD–REVISED EDITION

More than a decade ago we started to compile a catalogue of Flow Blue patterns with a description of the process of manufacture and the products thereof. Very few examples could be found. Most of the designs presented in the first book, published in 1971 were found in shops whose owners did not know or care about the blue dishes they held for sale. Some plates were found at personal sales and estate auctions, and some were bought by mail order from the sales list of an English supplier to the American antique trade. It was almost impossible to locate more than one example of most patterns, and therefore it was difficult to make comparable assessments of the colour printing. We admitted to our readers that errors were unavoidable, warned them to be careful when collecting Flow Blue, and apologized for the quality of the pictures which often were donated or taken at shows under difficult lighting conditions. Future research would have to wait upon the emergence of information after collectors became aware of the value and history of Flow Blue China, and started to correspond with each other and with us.

By good fortune this correspondence and interest grew steadily and much valuable information has been sent to us by collectors, interested researchers and antiquarians. We have tried to correct errors and amend descriptions in each of the three books that comprise the study, but as soon as we send a manuscript off to the printer, more new material starts to accumulate. Now we humbly acknowledge that it is improbable that we can or will ever accurately encompass the entire range of the field of Flow Blue China. It has been a great joy and satisfaction to realize that our books have brought knowledge and pleasure to so many people, and we are grateful to the Creator for the opportunity to do this work.

Now we end this latest work with the words of Simeon Shaw in conclusion of his book "History of the Staffordshire Potteries" (1829):

"It only remains to solicit indulgence for any inadvertencies, and corrections for an appendix, from every friend who can supply them."

Jeffersontown, Ky. January, 1981   Petra Williams

CONTENTS

INTRODUCTION

I.   A Simplified History of the Making of Pottery in Staffordshire, England.

The earliest pottery found in England is of a mortuary character; that is, it was found in tombs. Urns, cups, bowls, and incense pans have been discovered in grave mounds.

During the Roman occupation, crude pottery was still being made in Britain. Pieces have been found in excavations of old military camps. Jugs, pitchers, bowls, feeding bottles for infants were made, glazed only on the inside in order to retain liquids.

In the Fourteenth Century monks in various abbeys produced pottery. By the Sixteenth Century there were many such abbeys in or near Burslem, which later became the center of the Staffordshire potteries. This district in the northern part of Staffordshire about 150 miles northwest of London later was known as "The Potteries." These monasteries produced tiles to be used in buildings, and mugs, bowls, jugs, candlesticks, inkwells and tygs. Tygs are tulip shaped cups with one or two or three or more handles. They were passed around from drinker to drinker, each of whom drank from a different spot on the rim.

Henry the Eighth opposed Rome and the papal power and in so doing closed the monastaries of England in 1539. But much of the potters' art had been taught to laymen helpers, and they kept on producing wares for local use in Staffordshire. North Staffordshire is made up of many small towns: Tunstall, Brownhills, Longport, Burslem, Cobridge, Hanley and Shelton, Stoke, Fenton, Longton, Lane End, and Etrutia. Except for Longport all the above towns at the present day make up the city of Stoke-on-Trent. The Flow Blue collector will find these names or the initials of the above towns on the backstamps of a great many of his finds.

The potters who worked here owned small home potteries, and this art was part of the job of maintaining a household. Agriculture was the prime business of life, until coal and mining businesses developed.

Staffordshire had both coal and clay, equally necessary to make pots. Lead could be obtained from Lawton Park, six miles north. History relates that a William Adams of Tunstall was fined for digging clay from the road near his house in 1448.

In 1600 the landholders of Burslem and Tunstall became independent when the crown lands were split into copyholds and then given to the holders. These were small parcels of land, not suitable for farming as such. The potters had the opportunity to be secure and make a living other than from the land. Legal documents of the period begin for the first time to describe men as potters (1616).

These men made their pots in sheds next to their houses; they dug their own clay, and some dug their own coal. It was a peasant industry. A few pieces were made for show, little cradles to give to newlyweds, and puzzle jugs that were almost impossible to drink from without spilling. They also made clay pipes and elongated urns in which butter was taken to market.

A pile of clay, about three feet high was kept outdoors in rain, shine and cold for about a year. The rain washed away impurities, the cold hardened the clay, and the sun helped dry it. The shack in which the clay was fired was covered with turf to keep in the heat. The oven was beehive shaped and was about eight feet high and six feet wide. Next to this would be an open area in which to dry the ware, and a sun-pan, a long rectangular shallow tank. Part of the tank was deeper than the rest and in this the clay was beaten on flagstones until thoroughly mixed with water.

Then it was poured through a sieve into the sun-pan. When it was of the right consistency it was brought to a beating board and beaten with a wooden paddle until well mixed. The next step was to form the clay into rolls on a wageing board. The rolls were cut with a wire into slices and these were kneaded into balls and taken to the wheel, where the potter threw the clay and made it by hand into the shape he desired. The piece was set outside on a rack to dry, and in inclement weather was placed indoors by the fire. When dry it was painted with various kinds of slip, a clay mixture the consistency of syrup, which could be applied in various ways to make patterns. The slip decoration completed, the ware was leaded; that is, lead dust was sifted over the vessel. The dust, after firing, would give a glaze. The piece was now ready for the oven. It would be placed in a sagger, a covered box made of fire clay in order to protect it from the direct flame; each piece was separated from the one above it by three little pieces of clay which later became known as stilts. The oven was loaded from the bottom up, and when filled it was fired for 24 hours, then cooled for 10. The finished ware was removed from the kiln and consigned to cratemen to sell. These men carried the vessels on their backs and took them to packmen who traveled all over England on horseback.

In about 1690 two brothers from Holland, Elers by name, came to work in the district. They possessed the secret off-salt glazing. This was done by casting salt on the wares while the ovens were red hot. The saggers were perforated, and the vapor of the sodium chloride entered them. This reacted and with the water formed hydrochloric acid, which escaped and left a silicate of soda on the ware forming a layer of soda glass. The surface of the vessel resembled the pitted skin of an orange. This salt glaze was used (and is still used) on common clays and to produce stoneware.

The Elers brothers were artisans who had been silversmiths in Cologne and possessed great skill with a lathe, turning out delicate, beautifully finished red pottery. Their work was spied upon and soon the potters of Burslem had learned their secrets and followed their example. In 1693 Aaron Wedgwood is recorded as making stoneware.

The old method of making pots in the backyard had started to change. The open pan had been superseded by locked, indoor, heated troughs in which the clay was mixed in secret. But right up until today men are jiggers and jolliers and scallopers. Jiggers and jolliers shape pottery on a turntable and scallopers cut indentations around the rims.

Demand for more sophisticated goods caused demand for the development of molds. At first, in about 1730, alabaster was brought from Derbyshire. Blocks were cut and carved into patterns from which clay molds were made. Then in 1745 Ralph Daniel brought from France the secret of plaster of Paris. It must be remembered that Chinese porcelain of all shapes was being imported into the country and the Staffordshire potters had to compete against this for the market. Mold casting provided the answer. The liquid clay was poured into the mold, and let stand for a while, and then the excess was poured off. The shell that was left and removed when dry, could be delicate and decorative if the potter was skillful. Of course the great skill was that of the carver of the mold, the "block cutter." The most famous of these was Aaron Wood who worked in secret in a locked room.

In 1720 John Astury introduced ground flint and white Devonshire clay into the body of his ware and was able to fire at a higher temperature. Enoch Booth at

Tunstall invented a fluid lead glaze that gave eathenware a cream colour. The ware was dipped after firing, and then refired to fuse the glaze. Booth used Astury's white body ware for this process. In 1761 Josiah Wedgwood added Cornwall stone and developed Creamware. This was softly glazed, more servicable, and better looking than stoneware, and soon superseded the latter. Wedgwood did not patent his process, but gave it to all.

All of these changes in production culminated in the change from a peasant industry into a factory business. Capital was necessary to pay the skilled workmen, to advertise and distribute the finished goods and to develop even newer methods of production. In 1743 Thomas and John Wedgwood had five ovens; in 1762 we learn from a letter of Josiah Wedgwood that there were 500 potteries in or near Burslem and that they employed 7,000 people. At that time the ware had to be sent by carriage via the turnpikes from Burslem to the Mersey River at Winsford, or to the Trent River at Willington, in order to be shipped to Liverpool. When the 93 mile Mersey and Trent Canal was completed in 1777, it was possible to ship goods to and from the sea at Liverpool for one-seventh the cost of earlier methods.

The Staffordshire potteries had become one of the great industries of England.

In 1813 Charles James Mason took out a patent for "Ironstone China." This used the scoria (slag) of ironstone pounded in water, clay, and oxide of cobalt. According to Wooliscroft and Arca, ironstone was hard enough that it could be used for bedposts, large punch bowls, and cisterns as well as the usual wares such as dinner services, vases, and teapots. In 1851 the entire business of Mason was sold to Frances Morley and moved to Hanley, and then in 1862 was resold to George Ashworth & Bros. who carried on the Mason name and the Ironstone China mark.

It is the ware we call earthenware that was used — and still is used — to make the ware that is transfer printed in blue under the glaze.

Remember that pottery is opaque. You cannot see the shadow of your hand through it, light does not pass through it. On the other hand porcelain is translucent. Light does pass through it. A piece of earthenware may be heavy or it may be rather delicate and light, but no matter what the backstamp reads, "Real Ironstone," "Opaque China," "Semi-Porcelain," "Porcelain Opaque," "China Stone," "Oriental Stone," "Stone China," "Granite China," "Stone Ware," "Granite Ware," or "Kaolin Ware," these are all just different names for the same hard earthenware that was and is used for transfer printing and our Flow Blue.

Transfer printing on pottery (and on porcelain) had been developed about 1775 at Battersea, and by Sadler & Green at Liverpool. Before this, china had been decorated by hand with paint, colored enamels, and the like; painting was done by girls at the potteries and enameling was effected by special artists in thier own workshops. For example, Josiah Wedgwood used the Widow Warburton to enamel his ware, but after the invention of transfer printing he sent his goods to Sadler & Green in Liverpool. We find that he went there to supervise this, and to see about importing clay and exporting his wares to his overseas clients. America was fast becoming a large market.

In transfer printing, a metal plate, most often copper, was engraved with the desired pattern, and the cutting was done rather deeply. The colour to be used in the design was rubbed into the lines of the warmed plate, excess paint was removed from the plate with a palette knife and then the surface was wiped clean with a cloth called a boss. A piece of specially-made tissue paper was dampened and put over the copper plate. A print was forced on the paper by an ordinary plate press. The printed paper was lifted from the copper and carefully placed on the vessel to be decorated, rubbed down by the women called "Transferers" who used soft-soaped flannel. These women were responsible for placing the pattern correctly, for joining the seams of the borders and designs, and for applying the backstamp.

The ware was then placed in water; the paper floated off and the colour remained. The piece was slightly heated to dry the colour, and then was dipped into a glaze. It is of interest that the pattern disappeared at this point only to reappear after firing and the glaze had become transparent and glasslike.

Some of the artists who made the designs for the copper plates became famous. Thomas Minton did the original Willow pattern for Turner of Caughley. He invented the pattern and used oriental motifs but his pattern did not have the elements of the Fable. He drew two people on a bridge, no apple tree, no doves, and used conventional Chinese features, in a successful attempt to make a good composition in the round. This pattern was copied in various forms by the other potters, and is still in use today. The Willow story was unknown to the Chinese and is merely a romantic tale of the plight of a pair of lovers, she the daughter of a rich mandarin, and he, her father's employee. Her father locked her up because he wanted her to marry a rich man. She watched the willow tree blossom and the peach tree bud, then she and her sweetheart exchange love notes. He managed to free her and they escaped by boat to a little island where he had a small house. They lived happily a short time, then the rejected rival found their hideaway, and set fire to their home and the grove in which they were hiding. They died among the bamboo trees; from their ashes arose two white doves who hover above the scene of their earthly happiness.

Only the biggest firms could hire their own artist engravers. The smaller companies were supplied by engraving firms. According to Geoffrey Godden in his book, "Antique Glass and China," several firms would use the same design, with the individual initials changed for each. Many manufacturers purchased their designs from such firms as Sargeant and Pepper of Hanley who specialized in designing printed patterns, and engraved the copper plates necessary for printing. A popular design would be sold to several firms and the same mark design would be used, but different purchaser's initials would be engraved on it. Goddard cites "Asiatic Pheasants" and "Pekin" as two of the popular designs. Asiatic Pheasants was sold to more than twenty companies. This would explain the duplication of designs that appear in Flow Blue under different names, as each pottery chose its own title. This also explains the duplication of names, used for different designs. Duplication also occurred when a factory went bankrupt and was sold; the buyer would use the same name and pattern but would add his own factory mark. Copper plates carried the pottery mark of the factory producing the ware. When the paper was pulled from the plate, the name mark was cut off and slapped on the back of a plate or the bottom of a hollow piece. Sometimes this was omitted, and we get unmarked pieces.

Chinese trade porcelain had always been popular in blue, and the Chinese Nankin ware that was being imported in 1780-1820 was in dark blue; therefore, the Staffordshire potters printed in underglaze blue too. The deep blue was first used in Holland on Delftware. Holland traded earlier with the Orient than England and copied the blue of the Oriental ware.

In 1784 Josiah Spode printed Minton's Willow plate in blue and in 1787 Adams started his English and American views series in blue. The other great potters followed suit. (Wood, Clews, Tams, Ridgway, Rogers, Meigh, Hall, and Riley.) Blue had been used from the first also because blue from cobalt was the only color certain to survive the high temperature of the glaze process. This rich dark blue which we associate with the famous historical plates and which was used for early Flow Blue was prepared from cobalt oxide. This had been discovered in Saxony in 1545 by Schurer. He processed the cobalt oxide and named one of the products Zaffre and a finer one Smalt. This blue sank into the porous ware and then blurred a bit in the glazing period, thus giving a softness to the finished product.

In the 1820s it was discovered that although the blue would blur naturally, it could be made to flow by instilling lime or chloride of ammonia in the sagger while glazing. This deep blurring covered printing faults and stiltmarks and served to hide other defects such as glaze bubbles. Some of the pieces so made are so flown that it is impossible to discern border detail or center pattern; and some are done so lightly that only a halo effect appears. Other colors were used to make flowing ware — puce, mulberry, sepia — but blue was by far the most popular. It is of interest that the cobalt was brown when applied. The blue appeared after firing.

Which brings us to our own subject of Flow Blue. In order to recognize and collect this china, it is wise to be able to read the backstamp, or the impressions on the backs of plates and the bottom of holloware, and also to be able to recognize a pattern by its distinctive border and center design.

The back stamp usually gives the pattern name and the initials or the name of the maker, and quite often the town where the factory is located. But sometimes it is not this easy. If the initials are obscured, or the potter's name is not included, it is up to the collector to figure out the answers. A fascinating plate that you have found and that you feel, from the stilt marks and pattern genre, could date 1845-1850, is worth more to you as a collector if you know who made it and what pattern it is. (Stilt marks are three little dots in the glaze made by the triangular spur pieces which separated the plates in the kiln, and appear on early ware. On later ware they may appear faintly on the bottom but seldom on the face.)

Of course, you must realize that there were so many makers of opaque china, and enormous amounts of it sold, that it is not possible to identify all the marks; some potters stayed in business a very short time and made few pieces.

Marks can be applied in many fashions: first by scratching the green ware (the word 'green' does not denote the color of the body to be fired; it is used in the way we say wood is green before it is dried for the fire); second, by impressing a stamp into the soft body such as the Davenport anchor, or Rosette; third, by painting the information on the surface before or after glazing; fourth, by using a transfer stamp mark that is applied at the same time as the pattern and baked into the glaze kiln. A stamp can be used after glazing, but for the purpose of Flow Blue identification this should not be important unless you suspect a piece to be a fraud.

Printed marks outnumber all the others. In the case of Flow Blue the mark and pattern was transferred to the plate at the same time in cobalt blue. Marks that include the name of the pattern date after 1810. Victorian quarter arms date after 1837; round and oval garter marks date from 1840. The name "England" was used after 1875 and used extensively after 1891. The words "Made in England" date after 1900. The word trademark dates after 1862, and the word "Limited (Ltd.)" usually after 1880.

English china sometimes bears a diamond-shaped registry mark. This was used from 1842 until 1883; this signifies that the factory registered its pattern and would have rights to it for three years from the date. But the fact that the pattern was registered at a certain date does not mean that the piece so marked was made at that time. Factories used the marks for years afterwards in many cases. On January 1, 1884, the English Patent Office started to register patterns in consecutive numbers, beginning with number 1. The following figures, in round numbers were reached in the years given: 246,975 by 1895; 351,202 by 1900. In 1909, near the end of the period of this study, the number was 555,000. You can find this system of registration set forth in the mark books of Cushion and of Godden.

POTTERY IN THE UNITED STATES AND IN HOLLAND

Pottery in the American Colonies started with the founding of Jamestown, Virginia. By the time of Queen Victoria, American factories were turning out china at a fair rate. At first they copied the British wares, even to the point of copying the British coat of arms as a backstamp, because the American family wanted the best and considered the English china the most excellent. This prejudice slowly was discarded and the American ware became accepted. In our field of Flow Blue, Mercer in New Jersey, Wheeling Pottery Company in Wheeling, West Virginia, and Burgess & Campbell in New Jersey were among many who turned out services and bedroom sets. You can find American pottery marks in the mark books of Hazel Hartman and Kovel, and C. Jordan Thorn. (See bibliography). These books also contain European mark identification. But we note that as late as 1902, Montgomery Ward was advertising china from England.

In 1891 the American Congress passed the McKinley Tariff Act, and from then on wares that were to be imported to this country had to be marked with the country of origin, so if you see "England," "Holland," "Japan" and so on, you will realize that the piece dated after 1891. In some few cases English ware was marked "England" before this date, but as a rule of thumb you can apply this knowledge in your collecting.

One of the outstanding names in our field is that of Petrus Regout who founded his factory at Maastricht, Holland in 1834, from 1850 on we find transfer printed patterns in cobalt with his name or his initials. In 1879 the company took the name of Petrus Regout & Company and adopted a sphinx as its mark. Before this time, he sometimes used the coat of arms of the City of Maastricht, and sometimes a crowned knotted rope.

Another factory was founded in Maastricht in 1859. This was named the Societe-Ceramique, and produced blue transfer ware also.

These two factories were joined in 1958 with the name of N. V. Koninglijke (Royal) Sphinx-Ceramique. They closed their earthenware section in 1968.

INTRODUCTION

II. Methods Used In This Book To Aid Identification Of Flow Blue China

We will divide the era of Flow Blue production into three periods, and since Queen Victoria was on the throne of England during the same round of years, we will use the years of her reign as our time guide. Victoria reigned from 1837 until 1901.

Flow Blue was first discovered and made right after 1825, but production of more than just a few odd pieces did not start until after 1835. Therefore our periods will be:

Early Victorian, 1835-1840 — 1850s
Mid Victorian, 1860s-1870s
Late Victorian 1880s, 1890s, and the early years of the 1900s.

We will use 1910 as a cut off date. Many patterns that are favorite collectors items date around 1905 and 1906. You will find the letters: "E.V.", "M.V.", and "L.V.", referring to these Victorian periods on each classification in the main part of this book. The earliest examples that we find circa 1840 are predominantly Oriental. However the impact of the popularity of the British and American Historical views was still prevailing, therefore we find some scenic designs in the early flow pieces. But these views are not realistic or pictorial in the sense that they represent photographic drawings of the topography of a particular place as the earlier Historical had, instead they are romanticized versions of foreign scenes. Even bucolic country scenes were embellished with sentimental accents. Wakefield labels the Scenics as "purest fantasy, which taken as a group, provide an intimate image of early Victorian ideals." It could not be put better. Another writer speaks of the Elizabethan and Gothic Romanticism of the Victorians.

The Oriental views were also unrealistic. We find an East-Indian-Chinese sort of mixture. The elements of willow, bamboo, palm and apple trees, tea houses, pagodas, temples with upturned roofs, bridges, porches, towers, and little costumed people, were all put together to form a pleasing design. Prunus Blossoms, which are the flowers of the peach, almond, cherry and plum tree, are used extensively. Some artists used elements of the willow story as outlined in the Introduction of this book.

Borders on the early plates were stylized Far-Eastern designs; some were Arabic, and some contained small medallions with repeats of the motif of the center scene. Chinoiserie, combined with rococo had been the rage of the mid-eighteenth century, and we find a revival of this in transfer pottery one hundred years later in 1850-60.

Some floral patterns appear among the early pieces, but they are rare. When made, they were designed with restraint and realistic taste. (See Claremont Groups.)

The Mid-Victorian period was a time of great eclecticism and excessive ornamentation. That is, the designers borrowed from many different sources and mixed many diverse elements. We find Oriental plates with European flowers in the borders, and even Oriental scenes with Gothic borders. Baroque, extravagantly decorated borders, with irregularly shaped panels outlined by scrolls are fairly common. Rococo designs that evolved from the Baroque give us ornaments of shellwork and foliage. These appear predominantly in floral motif patterns. We find cartouche forms in the border designs. These are a series of medallions framing a small scene or a bouquet. Added to all this happy hodgepodge we sometimes discover elements of the classical school, such as statues, columns, wreaths, and large imposing urns filled to overflowing with trailing ferns and flowers.

The late Victorians were influenced by two famous writers. One was the poet and designer, William Morris (1834-1896), who invented the chair that bears his name. Morris loved the Medieval Ages and its cathedrals. The other man was Charles Eastlake. In 1865 he wrote a series of articles for the Queen magazine. These articles were brought together in a book that was still selling steadily in 1878. He was knighted in 1898 and died in 1906. Eastlake was an architect and a designer. He thought, and wrote, that gilding on china was vulgar, and fancy handles and knobs, silly, and of poor design. He said "In an age of debased design, the simplest style will be the best. The highest artistic qualities which can be associated in ceramic manufacture are beauty and vigor of form through harmony of color and propriety of ornament." We see Art Nouveau designs appearing at this point. This was a style of fine and applied art characterized by curvilinear motifs derived from natural forms of flowers and plants. This is stylized nature, and the late-Victorians liked stencils that gave this effect. Japanese art of this style was influential at this time also.

Through the last phase of Flow Blue production, floral transfer printed plates appeared by the thousands. Some were printed just on the rim, and some filled the plate. They were inexpensive to make and customers liked the varieties of buds, flowers, and sprays; this is the china we find predominantly at the close of our time period.

We will divide the patterns into the above-described classifications and a few others and they will appear as listed:

Oriental

Scenic

Floral

Art Nouveau

Miscellaneous (for those that defy classification
or combine two or more of the above types.)

In almost every case I have been able to state a date for the example shown. This has been effected by tracing the factory and the mark used by that factory at a certain period. Marks were changed periodically by manufacturers. My dating will read c. 1900 or c. 1860. "C" stands for "circa" which means around 1900 or around 1860.

The mark numbers are those used by Geoffrey Godden in his definitive work, "Encyclopedia of British Pottery and Porcelain Marks." These you can look up in the library, or if you are fortunate, in your own copy of his book. There appears at the end of this chapter an illustrated list of some of the marks which appear most often on Flow Blue China, each identified with the number Godden assigned to it. The registry number refers to the English registration series of numbers in the Introduction.

The early Victorian period saw the production of many panelled plates. These were not scalloped, but were made with 12 or 14 straight sides. The rim is divided by the mould into panels that run straight from edge to well. The well is the center part of a plate. Holloware, such as teapots, sugar bowls and pitchers were sometimes made in octogonal shapes, the sides were squared off vertically and were not rounded. You will find these shapes date, for the most part, from the same time as the early 12 sided plates.

In almost all cases the pattern name listed is given as printed on the mark. However, in a few cases, which you will find noted, I have used a descriptive name for the pattern because no pattern name has been found. (Note, "Vine" by Davenport)

Below is the list of marks which appear most often on Flow Blue.

Henry Alcock	Godden	Mk. 66	
Davenport	Godden	Mk. 1184	
Ford & Son	Godden	Mk. 1585	
W. H. Grindley	Godden	Mk. 1842	
Johnson Bros.	Godden	Mk. 2177	
J & G Meakin	Godden	Mk. 2600	
New Wharf Pottery	Godden	Mk. 2886	
Ridgways	Godden	Mk. 3313	
Wood & Son	Godden	Mk. 4285	

III. The Varieties Of Victorian China

Tea was introduced from China by the British East India Trading Company. Tea did not taste good in pewter, which had been used for ale, so the English copied the Chinese fashion and used cups, handleless cups, because the Chinese and India peoples poured the tea into a saucer and drank from that. Cup plates were soon invented to hold the (put-aside) cup. These were always made of earthen ware, not of porcelain, and were used from 1765 until about 1850. After that they were made of glass. In America, glass cup plates were made from 1825 on. According to Kamm at first cup plates were about four inches, but after 1825, they were made smaller. Few of these are marked. The tea ceremony called for new and different ware.

TEA SERVICE

Handleless cups	Creamer
Milk pitcher	Milk pitcher
Cup plates	Cake plates
Tea pot	Tea plates
Sugar bowl	Waste bowl

You may be lucky and come across a little dish that is larger than a cup plate which has a deep well. This could be a preserve pot lid and was used on top of a crock weighted down with a stone put in the well.

Sugar bowls were very large until the middle 1860s. Sugar was, and is, made by cutting cane or beets into small sections, and crushing and grinding the pieces between toothed rollers. The leftover pulp is used for fuel. The remaining juice is mixed with lime and heated to the boiling point, and during this process, the insoluable compounds mix with the lime and can be filtered off along with the other impurities. The remaining "massecuite," consisting of sugar crystals and syrup was reboiled and poured into conical molds which resembled rounded clown's hats. These molds had a hole in the end and the excess syrup ran out. At this point in European refineries, a process known as claying took place. A mixture of clay and water was poured into the mold, and percolated through the sugar particles carrying off the remaining impurities and syrup. This left a fairly white sugar which is today called "first" sugar or "raw" sugar. When the sugar was dry, the mold was broken, and a sugar loaf, cone shaped, remained. Loaves weighed about five pounds.

Until about 100 years ago the housewife purchased these loaves wrapped in deep blue paper, and used sugar nippers to cut off pieces to be placed in her large wide-mouthed sugar basin or bowl. Sugar tongs were used on the table to lift the lumps from bowl to cup.

Later the process of granulating the sugar crystals was developed. The raw sugar was re-dissolved, de-colored, and re-crystalized into the more desirable size thus ending the need for the large sugar bowl.

VARIETIES OF VICTORIAN CHINA

Cheese dishes	Egg Cups	Jardiniers	Pin trays
Butter dishes	Egg Drainers	Candlesticks	Bureau trays
Bone dishes	Baskets for Egg Cups	Hat pin holders	Shaving mugs

Chamber pots
Biscuit jars
Individual oval vegetables
Pickle dishes
Spoon trays
Picture plates (to hang)
Butter pats
Potato or berry bowls
Footed custard cups with handles
Punch cups
Salt dishes
Gravy boats with trays
Compotes
Wall pocket vases (cornucopias)
Hot water plates
(pewter well bottoms)
Soup tureens with trays
Ladles
Sauce tureens with stands
Toy sets of dishes
Toy tea sets
Mugs
Dinner plates
Chargers (to hang on wall
or stand on shelf)

Pie plates
Cereal dishes
Round serving dishes
Oval serving dishes
Nappies
Pitchers, 1 pt., 1 qt., 2 qt.
Covered vegetable dishes
Covered casseroles
Platters
Sauce boats
Soup plates with flange rims
Flat soups
Pickle dishes
Covered butters with drainers
Ewers
Tiles
Pitchers
Basins
Toothbrush holders
Soap dishes
Chop plates
Vases
Chocolate pots
Chocolate cups
Coffee cups

WARD'S CATALOG 1902
"Flow Blue Peach Blossom Pattern"
(Service for twelve)
All for $15.79

Tea cups/saucers (handled)
Coffee/saucers (handled)
Pie plates
Tea plates
Breakfast plates
Dinner plates
7" Soups
4" Fruit sauce dishes
Oatmeal bowl
Oyster bowl — 1 pint
Bone dishes
Individual butters
Bowl (1-1/2 pint)

Platters, 16", 14", 12", 10", 8"
Nappies 8"
Pitchers, 1 pt., 1 qt., 2 qt.
Covered vegetable dish 8"
Covered casserole 8"
Soup tureen with ladle
Sauce tureen, ladle and stand
Sauce boat
Pickle dish
Cake plate
Tea pot
Covered butter
Sugar and creamer

Oriental Category

AMOUR

Societé Céramique

This pitcher is printed in a very dark shade with a typical oriental floral border and the well is outlined with a small stylized floral edging.

The center scene shows an overscaled blooming peony tree at left. The tree peony was called by the Chinese the "King of Flowers", and was revered, and planted in raised flower beds. A turretted tea house, situated on a rocky island, is at the right, and a pennant is flying from its tower. A bridge connects it to the garden and the peony tree. Under the bridge there is a boat with a flag and in the boat stands a man holding a pole.

Dutch, marked as above, M.V., c 1865

AMOY

made by Davenport

These plates are twelve sided and paneled and their edges have a crosshatched border. Cartouche forms alternate with flower groupings around the rims. The printing is very dark.

The center scene shows at left two mandarin figures in peaked tasselled hats. One is seated and holds a fringed parasol, the other leans on a garden fence as they converse. The flowers about them are typically oversized.

Amoy is a Chinese port city not far from Hong Kong.

English, Impressed anchor mark, Mk. 1181A, E.V., dated 1844

12

BAMBOO

made by Thomas Dimmock

This dish has sixteen panels, but it does not have flat side edges. The outer edge has a border of small fleur-de-lis. The rim is printed with sprays of prunus and chrysanthemums.

The center design consists of two over-scaled flowers, and two bamboo stalks topped with clusters of leaves. In the foreground is stylized grass.

English, marked "D" and "Kaolin Ware", Mk. 1298, E.V., c 1845

BEAUTIES OF CHINA

made by Mellor, Venables & Co.

The soup plate photographed is fourteen sided and is paneled. Its edge is detailed with printed straight lines that are contained in scrolls. The border design is composed of snail-like scrolls and formalized flowers. Small willow sprigs descend towards the center. The well is defined by a ring of rounded pebbles and foliated cartouches and stylized lotus blossoms.

The center scene shows a very tall rock and trees at left. (This could be a representation of a mountain.) In the center of the picture two men are standing on a bridge which leads to an island on which there are a pagoda and apple tree. In the background there is a lake, with two other islands, the island at upper right has a tall rock formation also.

English, and marked "Ironstone" in a semi circle, marked M. V. & Co., Mk. 2645, E.V. c 1845

BOMBAY

made by Thomas Furnival & Sons

The edge of this plate is decorated with basket weave. The border design consists of three hanging basket planters, each suspended by two cords from a ring; sprays of prunus trail from their tops and garland into the well. Between each basket is a nosegay of two flowers tied with a bow.

The center design is encircled by a ring of basketweave and consists of a bouquet of water lilies, lily pads and reeds.

English, marked as above, Mk. 1649, M.V., dated 1876

CANTON

made by John Maddock

These plates are twelve sided and paneled. The edge is outlined with a narrow band of geometric diaper pattern. The rim is printed with mock calligraphy in eight places. The well is outlined by a ¾" ring made of rounded floral motifs.

The center pattern is a large grouping that covers the well, and is a design of overscaled flowers and leaves.

English, marked Maddock (imp.) Mk. 2461, c 1850

CARLTON

made by Samuel Alcock

This plate is 12 sided and is paneled. There is a double row of embossing around the edge. The upper rim is printed in four places with an angled trellised fence. Below this are scrolls and flowers that form a wreath around the rim, and parts of these enter the well.

The center scene is of overscaled flowers; the one at left resembles lotus, and the one at right is a spray of mimosa type. These are divided by a fence that is angled to the right, then makes an S curve into the middle-ground. There are flower sprays on the reverse side of the rim.

English, makred S.A. & Co., Mk. 75, E.V. 1850

CASHMERE

made by Francis Morley

The border of this plate is printed with mauresque lambrequins and semi-floral forms and this design enters the well.

This pattern is famed for the center scene of two little deer, one has antlers, that confront each other with upraised front leg. Their background consists of the usual over-scaled flowers and leaves.

English, marked F. M. & Co., Mk. 2760, E.V., c 1850

CELESTE

made by W. & E. Corn

The small platter shown has a scalloped edge and its upper border is printed with a very dark field contained by scrolls and medallions. The lower rim is printed with bouquets of prunus, and these enter the well.

At right, in the center scene is a large figured urn filled with overscaled dahlias. At its base is a rocky arch and an overscaled flower with leaves. At left there are a small teahouse, large stylized rocks and a tree. A bridge joins the two elements of the design. On the bridge there are two figures, one is carrying a sunshade.

English, marked with *, L.V., c 1900*

(This mark appears on a pattern named "Ayr" and another plate in this same pattern was marked W. & E. Corn. This was also true of other Corn designs.) This mark also appears on dishes marked "Superior, Germany."

CEYLON

made by Thomas Furnival & Sons

The outer edge of this plate is decorated with a border of criss-cross, and quatrefoils. There are branches of prunus and a butterfly in three places on the rim, separated by a stylized floral snow flake type figure.

The well is defined by a circle of snail-curve brocade and an inner row of dots.

The center design is a picture of a large, rounded, wide-lipped urn filled with over-scaled flowers and leaves. A willow tree is placed behind the jar. There is a small piece of fence at the left, and grassy hummocks are placed in the foreground.

English, marked as above, like Mk. 1649, M.V., c 1876

CHAPOO

made by John Wedge Wood

The plate shown is twelve sided and is paneled, and has a deep well. The edge is outlined by a narrow diaper printed border, the rim is decorated with two alternating patterns of stylized flowers, and the well is defined by a narrow ring of geometrical floral design.

The center scene depicts a large pagoda in the center right foreground. It is linked to an island at left by a small bridge. The usual tall flowering tree is in the center ground, and there are two small figures at the base of the tree. In the distance are three islands, two have buildings on them.

English, marked J. Wedgwood, Mk. 4276A, E.V., c 1850

CHEN-SI

made by John Meir

This plate is fourteen sided, paneled, and has a deep well. The border is printed in a very dark pattern of treillage (lattice design). Stylized flowers and rococo scrolls alternate over this border design. The well is outlined by a narrow band of diamond pattern.

The center scene shows a large pagoda at the right, which is surrounded by palm trees and a fence. Stairs descend from the building to the center front, and on the stairway are two little figures, the forward one is carrying a sunshade. Other stairs lead to a parapet at left, and there are large rocks and a flower tree behind the parapet. In the far center distance there is another building.

Chen Si is a town in Sinkiang, China.

English, marked I.M., Mk. 2632, E.V., c 1835

CHINESE

made by Thomas Dimmock

The edge of this plate is gently and unevenly scalloped. The upper border is printed with a fish scale design. On the rim six scroll-edged reserves that contain a stylized lotus and a little flower that is pendant from each. These alternate with six triangular scroll designs from which depend wild roses with sylized leaves and buds.

The center design is of a porch and a tall flowering tree at the left. In the right middle distance there is a tall feathery leaved tree and some rocks. In the far center ground there stands a garden house that has several platforms over a body of water. Two tiny figures, one with a parasol, are standing next to the house. The plate is printed in dark blue and overpainted with henna, a pinkish red, and other colors.

English, marked D., "Kaolin Ware," Mk. 1298, E.V., c 1845

CHINESE

made by Wedgwood

The border is indented at the edge of this plate and is printed with a design of flowers and scrolls, the bottom of which enters the well.

The center scene shows several small ornate gazebos that are situated on a lake, and at right is a sampan with sails. A tall flowering tree rises in the center to tower over the entire scene.

English, impressed Wedgwood, Mk. 4088, L.V., c 1908

CHINESE JAR

made by Thomas Green

The rim of this plate is paneled from edge to well and these panels are raised and rounded. The border is printed with cartouche forms that are linked by a basket weave edging.

The center scene is ringed by a characteristic Chinese diaper pattern, and depicts a large jar on a pedestal base, and the usual overscaled flowers.

English, marked T.G., (See Ormsbee, P. 64), Mk. 1, E.V., c 1855

CHINESS

made by Petrus Regout

This saucer has a slightly scalloped edge. The rim is printed with overscaled flowers, alternating with scrolls, which are headed by a treillage border design.

The center scene shows a girl holding a parasol. Beside her is a kneeling boy who is offering a dish of seed to a spread-tailed peacock. The usual oriental flowers, rocks and trees surround the figures.

Dutch, impressed P. Regout-Maastricht, E.V., c 1856

CHUSAN

made by J. Clementson

This twelve sided plate is paneled. The rim is printed with an edging of triangle diaper design and five scroll forms alternating with five scenes of a pavilion. The deep well is defined by a ring of the triangle patterns.

The center scene shows a small house at front which is linked to another structure at right rear by a fence. Near the first house at left center front stand two figures dressed in tunics and tiered skirts. At left middle distance is another building. The usual bamboo trees are included on both sides of the design. Two large birds dominate this design. They are flying at top center and probably represent the souls of the lovers of the "Willow Legend".

English, marked Ironstone, J. Clementson, Mk. 920A, E.V., c 1840

CHUSAN

made by Podmore Walker & Co.

The deep saucer photographed has sixteen small panels. The edge is outlined with a diaper pattern contained within scrolls. Small baroque cartouches alternate with double peonies around the rim.

The center scene shows a tea house at left. A bridge crosses from it to a garden of overscaled flowers, a tall tree and a parapet. Two little figures are on the bridge near the tea house, one is holding an instrument of two bells hanging from a "Y" shaped form, and the other is blowing a horn.

English, marked P.W. & Co. and impressed rosette. Mk. 3075, English E.V., c 1845

CHUSAN

made by Wedgwood

This plate is very gently scalloped and its border is outlined by small curved oriental designs. Twelve small flowers are evenly placed around the rim. The well is outlined with a picket design.

The center scene is dominated by an overscaled lotus tree at the left. In right middle distance there is a bridge leading to a small towered pagoda.

English, impressed, marked Wedgwood, Mk. 4075, c 1882

CIRCASSIA

made by J. & G. Alcock

The deep saucer photographed has sixteen panels, so we may assume that the plates in this pattern are sixteen sided and paneled. The edge is printed with a honeycomb and diamond diaper design. The rim is covered with arabesques of scrolls, and flowers and sprigs.

The center scene is of water and islands. On the islands are towered pagodas with porches, or railings, and steps. In the center foreground a sacred lotus tree rises from a rock garden to tower over the entire scene. (Circassia is in Russia, by the way, and not in China where the lotus tree grows.)

English, impressed Oriental Stone, marked J. & G. Alcock, Mk. 69, E. V., c 1840

CIRIS

could be Wood & Baggaley

This plate has an unevenly scalloped edge that is enhanced by a heavy embossed ridge that terminates in leaves at five evenly spaced points around the edge. The whole plate is covered with a pattern of overscaled flowers. In the left middleground there is a garden house and at left rear there is an arched bridge. At the extreme left, and on the rim, a bird is perched on a spray of prunus. In the right background there are two little buildings and some jagged symbols that represent rocks.

English, marked W. & B., Mk. 4239, M.V., c 1875

COREAN

made by Podmore Walker & Co.

The plate photographed is in flowing sepia. It has proved impossible to locate one in blue. However, Freeman lists this as a blue pattern. It is included so that the pattern may become familiar and recognized if found in blue.

The plate has twelve sides and is paneled and the border design consists of foliated cartouches. The deep well is defined by a fence-like circle.

The center scene is of a temple in the middle distance at left. This is situated on water and a pennant flies from its tower. In the foreground sits a little figure on a parapet. His hat is plumed and he is holding a tiered parasol. A large jar filled with overscaled flowers is at right, and a tall bamboo and palm tree rise behind the flowers to fill the middle top of the scene. A small boat, flying a flag, is at far distance right.

English, marked P.W. & Co., Mk. 3080, E. V., c 1850

EUPHRATES

made by William Ridgway

This fourteen sided paneled plate has a border printed in a combination of light blue moss background, with spaces left open to form reserves in which are printed a scene of mosques with domes and palm trees, in a dark blue.

The center scene shows tall date palms. In the foreground, a man is riding a camel and two figures are seated at the left of the trees. In the distance there are minarets and other Eastern buildings separated by a river, presumably the Euphrates in Turkey.

English, marked W. R., Mk. 3300, E. V., c 1834

FAIRY VILLAS (II)

made by W. Adams Co.

This plate is unevenly scalloped and the edge is defined by a diaper pattern of circles and bars. The rim design consists of groups of peonies that alternate with cartouche forms that contain bouquets on a point d'esprit background. This is the same border as that of Fairy Villas I, which is shown in the floral category. The well is defined by a chain of tiny flowers.

The center design shows a tea house with stairs at the right. At left is a fancy porch with an upcurved roof, and a figure holding a trident stands on the porch. In the background there is a body of water in which is placed a sailboat containing two figures. In the far center background are trees and a pagoda, and in the foreground are larger flowers.

English, marked W. Adams & Co., Tunstall, Mk. 31, L. V., c 1891

FAIRY VILLAS (III)

made by W. Adams & Co.

The border is the same as Fairy Villas I.

The center scene depicts a large teahouse with trees at the left. Steps from the house descend to the center and the door of the house is ajar. Seated on a railing that projects from the house is a small figure with a large hat. At right, is a rococo tower-like structure and trees. A robed figure stands here. In the center background there is water on which there is a sailboat with a figure in it. In the background beyond the water are buildings and trees, and in the distance there are mountains. In the center foreground there is a lawn and some flowers.

English, marked W. Adams & Co., Tunstall, Mk. 31, L. V., c 1891

(A reply from the Adams Co. was received in answer to my inquiry about why so many different transfer centers were used with the same border design over the years. The Fairy Villas pattern was used at the Stoke factory until 1864, and then taken over by a branch of the family operating at the Greenfields Works at Tunstall, and was used at the Greenfields and Greengates Works from 1890 to 1917. The letter states that the pattern was last made, as far as the factory can trace, until about 1930.)

FORMOSA

made by F. Jones

This plate is unevenly scalloped and has some leaf and scroll embossing at the edge. The rim is outlined with a border of small circles.

The entire plate is covered with a picture of a teahouse with a bridge at left that crosses water to an island on which there is a building. A figure is seated, fishing near the entrance to the bridge, and another person is crossing it. The usual overscaled flowers are placed around the scene and two large doves fly at top center.

English, mark blurred, could be F. J., Mk. 2215, M. V., c 1870

FORMOSA

made by Thos., John & Joseph Mayer

This plate has sixteen sides and is gently paneled. The border is printed in very deep blue with cartouche forms and lattice work. Five small spaces on the rim were left white and resemble birds.

The center scene shows a garden house and tall palm trees at center left. A boat is beached at center right with a woman seated in the prow, and a man stands behind her. This is probably taken from the "Willow Story" when the lovers fled by boat and escaped to his island cottage.

English, marked T. J. & J. Mayer, Mk. 2570, E. V., c 1850

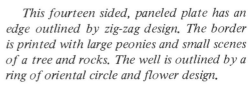

FORMOSA

made by W. Ridgway

This fourteen sided, paneled plate has an edge outlined by zig-zag design. The border is printed with large peonies and small scenes of a tree and rocks. The well is outlined by a ring of oriental circle and flower design.

The center scene shows a two storied house with a flared roof, which is situated on an island under a tall tree. Nearby at right, there is a standing man who is fishing. Another figure crosses a bridge at far right. In the background are several islands with trees, rocks, and buildings.

English, marked W. R., Mk. 3301, E. V., c 1834

GEISHA

made by Upper Hanley Potteries Ltd.

The gravy boat photographed has a scalloped and embossed edge.

The central design is of a seated geisha, holding a comb and mirror, attended by her standing maid. The border design repeats this vignette alternating with a baroque scroll design.

English, marked as above, Mk. 3929A, Reg. #254458 L. V., c 1901

HINDOSTAN

made by Petrus Regout

The border design on this plate is a narrow diapered band that connects oval cartouches containing stylized flowers. These are also linked with a lantern and bar design.

The entire well is covered with a scene which is dominated by a three-storied temple. Extending from this building to front center is a wide walkway, apparently over water. A bridge crosses left from the temple to a flowered, rocky island. In far left distance is another building, and at center right top is a stylized flowering tree.

Dutch, impressed, marked P. R., Maastricht, M. V., c 1860

HINDUSTAN

made by John Maddock

This plate is paneled and has fourteen sides. The rim is outlined with dark zig-zag edging. The border is printed with alternating lotus blossoms and buds, and rock-like forms with flowers.

The center scene, defined by a circle of oriental panel and floral diaper design, depicts two buildings connected by a bridge. At left is a turreted house surmounted by a finial. A figure stands between the house and bridge. A tall tree rises from the right bank. At left rear is an island on which stands a house. In the middle center ground there is a boat.

English, impressed, marked Ironstone China, Mk. 2461, E. V., c 1855

HONC

made by Petrus Regout

The edge of this plate is outlined by a small diamond design. The rim is printed with gothic forms that alternate with open areas in which are depicted small pagodas. The well is defined by a ring of blue strips and small formal scroll designs.

The center scene shows three persons, a seated mandarin, a child, and a woman holding a large sunshade. A tall flared-roofed temple is in the background at right, and a tall palm tree rises at center right. At left there is a sampan on which a man is standing holding a pole. At left, far distant, are other tall buildings.

Dutch, impressed, marked P. Regout, Maastricht, E. V., c 1858

HONG

made by P. & G.

This small deep welled plate may be a preserve jar top. The well is deep and straight sided (not sloped) and the bottom ring is 3/8" deep. The border is covered with a floral and scroll design that alternates with a geometric diapered panel.

The center scene is of flowers and at left is a small monument, and at right front is a double domed cylindrical structure.

Probably English, no mark found, E. V., c 1850

HONG KONG

made by Charles Meigh

This fourteen sided, paneled dish has an edge that is outlined by very dark triangular marks and reserves with half circles. The border is covered with stylized lotus flowers. The well is deep, and is outlined by a herringbone design that rises onto the rim

The center scene shows three small islands with houses. A bridge crosses left center front to a stylized cliff and there are two tiny figures on the bridge. One is carrying a pole and line. Five little birds fly in upper center.

English, marked Improved Stone China, Mk. 2618, E. V., c 1845

INDIAN

could be made by F. & R. Pratt

This fourteen sided paneled plate has an edge that is decorated with small four-pointed stars that are set in a spade shaped outline. The border is printed with sprays of dahlia-like flowers. The well is defined by fourteen inverted scalloped ridges.

The center scene is of a fence and a stone stair shaped monument, and tall flowering trees with overscaled flowers. At left is a tree with large prunus blossoms.

The mark on the backstamp is an oblong with oriental marking. Serry Wood in "China Classics, Vol. 6" Pg. 76, attributes this plate to Cauldon and dates it after 1882. Pratt used this mark also. Only part of the mark shows on this plate.

English, could be Mk. 3144, E. V., c 1840

INDIAN JAR

made by Jacob & Thos. Furnival

The platter photographed is basically octagonal, but it has twelve straight sides. It is paneled and has a diaper border enclosed by feather scrolls and open oval cartouche forms. The well is defined by ¾" deep ring of brocade and medallion design.

The center scene is dominated by a rounded urn at left. This stands on a tall base and is surmounted by two small jars. At right are overscaled peonies and a lotus tree. All of the elements are placed on a fanciful platform made of scrolls.

English, marked J. & T. F., Mk. 1644, E. V., c 1843

INDIAN STONE

made by E. Walley

The pitcher shown is paneled, as are the plates in this pattern. The border is composed of stylized floral patterns.

The center design is dominated by a handled urn filled with overscaled flowers. On either side of the urn are smaller stylized flowers.

English, marked W., Mk. 3990, E. V., c 1850.

Also marked with urn & scroll "Cobridge".

JAPAN

made by Sampson Bridgwood & Son

This plate is printed in a pale greyish blue. The edge is gently scalloped and is outlined by a narrow scallop diaper pattern.

The border is printed with vignettes of buildings and palm trees, which alternate with drawings of square footed urns containing bouquets. These are separated by arabic forms that contain a lotus design.

The center scene is identical to Fair Villas II.

English, marked SB (wreath), Mk. 596, L. V., c 1900

JAPAN

made by Thos. Fell & Co.

This plate is twelve sided and is paneled. The rim is outlined with running scrolls. The border pattern is composed of rounded cartouche forms that alternate with sprays of stylized flowers.

The center scene shows an arched bridge, under which a tiny sail boat can be seen; there are pagodas and trees in the distance. In the foreground, at right, is a large urn filled with overscaled lotus blossoms. There are also flowers around the arch at left and at top left a butterfly soars over the scene.

English, marked T. F. & Co., Mk. 1534, M. B., c 1860

JAPANESE

could be Wood and Baggaley

The border of this saucer is decorated with semi-cartouches that enclose a fan shape and a diaper pebbled pattern; a small stylized flower hangs from these. The alternate pattern is composed of large foliated scrolls in which are centered single bell flowers.

The center picture shows a railing at left, behind which there is an overscaled lotus tree. There is a footed table at the right, on which there is an urn that has big handles, and which is filled with a pair of flowers and some sprigs. In the foreground there are stylized rock forms.

English, marked W. & B., Mk. 4239, M. V., c 1875

JEDDO

made by W. Adams & Son

This plate is printed in slate blue on a paneled fourteen side form. The rim is outlined by a scroll diaper pattern and chrysanthemums. The border is printed with four vignettes of an urn, fence and flowers. The well is defined by a dark ring and fleur-de-lis.

The center scene is of a large urn at right front. It is surrounded by the usual overscaled flowers, and a palm tree is at right middle distance. At the left is a towered pagoda, and in the center distance are small islands and a building.

"Jeddo" was probably a translation of the word Tokio. The Adams Co. used the same name later for a different pattern which is not oriental.

English, marked Ironstone, and as above, Mk. 22, E. V., c 1845

JEDDO

made by Brown-Westhead, Moore & Co.

The soup plate photographed has a rim design of semi-circular reserves, each containing a picture of Japanese inspiration; a man planting rice, cranes, houses with steep roofs and a fence, sparrows on a branch, and butterflies and flowers. These are joined by curved triangles that contain cloud lines. The well is defined by a circular band of snail scrolls and vertical bars.

The center is covered with a picture of a folding fan that is opened to show its flowered design of morning glories and a butterfly; its carrying ribbons swirl across the bottom of the well and end in little decorated balls.

English, marked B. W. M. & Co., Mk. 679, M. V., c 1865

KIN SHAN

made by Edward Challinor

This plate is fourteen sided and is paneled. The border is printed with alternating large lotus blossoms and a stylized design. The well is rimmed with a ½" edge of a fence design with gate-like openings.

The center scene has two pagodas linked across the middle by a bridge. The pagoda at left has a pennant flying from its tower. There are two figures dressed in long gowns on the bridge, one carries a parasol. A tall flowering tree is at left and rises to cover the top center. In far center distance are other buildings.

English, marked E. C. & Co., Mk. 836, E. V., c 1855

KIRKEE

made by John Meir & Son

The edge of the saucer shown is outlined by a diamond pattern. The border design consists of a group of stylized flowers that alternate with a little scene of a man fishing from a porch. The center well is encircled by a brocade and medallion ring.

The center scene consists of five islands, each has a little house on it.

English, marked I. Meir, "Ironstone," Mk. 2639, M. V., c 1861

KYBER

*first made by John Meir & Son,
and later by W. Adams & Co.*

The plates in this set are twelve sided and paneled. The border is divided into five scrolled reserves, within each is depicted the same teahouse, rocks and tall trees. These are separated by a narrow fleur-de-lis design. The well is encircled by a brocaded rim that is edged toward the center with a picket pattern.

The center scene shows a porch that has scrolled railings. On the porch one person is seated holding a sunshade, the other is standing and serving from a low table. At left is a tall pagoda and a bamboo tree, and at right is a large stylized urn and flowers.

English, marked I. Meir and Son, Mk. 2639, M. V., c 1870 and marked W. Adams & Co., like Mk. 31, L. V., c 1891

LAHORE

made by W. & E. Corn

This plate has a gently scalloped rim outlined with a dark band. The border has four groups of stylized flowers and an urn design, separated by triangular stylized lotus blossoms. The well is outlined by a dark band that has a picot stitch halo effect.

The center scene is dominated by a large urn at center right. This is framed by curving tree branches. At left are towered pagodas.

English, marked ⟨W⟩, L. V., c 1900

LAHORE

made by Thos. Phillips & Son

The plates in this set are fourteen sided and are paneled.

The pitcher shown has a collar that is the same as the border on the plates. Oval cartouches, framed in foliated scrolls alternate with bouquets of lotus blossoms and buds. The well is defined on the plates by a diapered ring.

At right, in the center scene, is a large towered pagoda with a garden house that is situated on water. In the middle center distance there is a small boat. Bamboo trees are at left. In the foreground there are two figures standing on a parapet. A behatted man, in a kimona, is pointing toward the boat, and a smaller person, who is coiffed in a veil, stands next to him. A large flower is at their right and there are a vase and table at left.

Lahore is a district capitol city in Pakistan, India.

English, marked T. Phillips & Son Burslem, Mk. 3016A, E. V., c 1840

LINTIN

made by Thos. Godwin

This plate is twelve sided and is paneled. The rim design is of arabic-arch-formed scrolls and fish-scale diaper panels. These are separated by a stylized flower with sprigs.

The center scene depicts a tall gate with a fancy roof, a tower surmounted with a scrolled epi, and with fences that run to the left and to the right rear. In the distance there are other towers with pennants. These towers are connected by a bridge. In the foreground are flowers, a little fence, and at the right a pair of swans are swimming.

"Lintin" is the name of an island in the Pearl River at the approach to Canton, and was well known to sailors in the China Trade.

Thomas Godwin potted by himself only from 1834 to 1854.

English, marked T. G., Mk. 1729, E. V., c 1845

MADRAS

made by Doulton & Co.

The edge of this plate is rimmed for about 1/3" with a typical oriental geometric pattern. The rim is printed with alternating flowers and temples. The well is defined by a wide band of brocade patterns.

The center scene depicts a large ornate pagoda at the right that is situated on water. A typical tall graceful tree rises at left, and there are other pagodas at the left rear. Three little figures are in the foreground, two are standing and one is seated. At their side is a table with two levels, and an urn is on each surface.

English, marked Doulton, Burslem, Mk. 1832, L. V., c 1900

MALTESE

made by Cotton & Barlow

This plate is octagonal and is paneled. The border is decorated with stylized peonies and lotus flowers. The edge is defined by a trellised diaper pattern and the deep well has a thick circle of brocade around its outer edge.

The center scene is of two pagodas that are linked with a bridge.

English, Cartouche mark C. & B. L., could be Mk. 1116, E. V., c 1850

MANDARIN

made by Pountney

This platter has a slightly scrolled gadroon edge and the border is printed with geometric oriental designs that enclose fish-scale diaper patterns.

The center design shows a town. There re many houses, and at right center, in the window of the largest house stands a man holding a sceptre. There is a stream in the center of the scene and a small boat floats below the mandarin's window. In the distance a little figure crosses a bridge. Depicted are flowers and trees, boats in the water, and wave-like forms that denote rocks.

English, marked Pountney, Mk. 3112, L. V., c 1900

MANILLA

made by Podmore Walker

The border on this twelve sided paneled plate has alternate large lotus flowers and pictures of a little teahouse with steps. The well is outlined with a border ring of cross-hatching and stylized lotus.

The center scene shows many little islands. In the foreground two figures are crossing a bridge, one carries a lantern on a pole. The bridge leads from an island teahouse and garden with tall weeping willow trees, to another island on which there is a pavilion.

English, impressed, marked P. W. & Co. "Stoneware," Mk. 3075, E. V., c 1845

NANKIN

made by F. & R. Pratt

This paneled plate has twelve sides. The border is detailed with small comb-tooth edging, and is covered with stylized flowers in the Chinese manner. The well is defined by a thick circle of woven reed design with small floral reserves.

The center scene shows a railed porch at left with a tall flowering tree behind it, and a large overscaled flower at the right.

English, marked F. & R. P. & Co., Mk. 3144, E. V., c 1840

NING PO

made by R. Hall & Co.

This fourteen sided plate has a paneled rim that is divided into five reserves, each showing the same temple with a wide stairway.

The center scene depicts a lady carrying a tea tray; she is ascending a flight of stairs to the left. At the top of the stairs there is a pagoda, and a figure is standing nearby. At right center is a teahouse built on a bridge, two tall palm trees and the usual large flowers.

English, marked R. H. & Co., Mk. 1890A, E. V., c 1845

OREGON

made by T. J. & J. Mayer

The plates in this pattern are fourteen sided and paneled with the rims outlined in very dark blue. The border design has six cartouche forms alternating with an urn shaped pattern. The deep well is circled by zig-zag lines and little diamonds.

The center scene depicts a man wearing a hat who is bearing a yoke with two containers. He is standing on a brick terrace facing a large open arch in which a basket of flowers is suspended. The arch is surmounted by an awning on poles with a pennant flying from its right side. There are typical overscaled flowers at the right.

English, marked "T. J. & J. Mayer", Mk. 2570, E. V., c 1845

ORIENTAL

made by Samuel Alcock

This gently scalloped plate has a rim o, rouge-de-fer (terra cotta red). Peonies .are printed over the red. The well is defined by a circle of diaper pattern that alternates with a formalized floral medallion. This pattern was also made without the red border, by the same maker.

The center scene is of an overscaled water lily and pad. Fences at right center enclose a yard in which tall bamboos grow.

English, marked S. A. & C., Mk. 75, E. V., c 1840

ORIENTAL

made by Empire Porcelain Co.

The plate shown has a border of pierced lattice work and embossed shells. The border is in a dark cobalt and the rest of the pattern is printed in a greyish blue.

The entire plate is covered with a variant design of the willow story.

English, marked "Empire", Mk. 1488, L. V., c 1900

ORIENTAL

made by New Wharf Pottery

This plate has the same border design as Ridgway's Oriental, but it is printed with a different shade of blue. It is scalloped and embossed with chains, beads and fleurs--de-lis.

A ring of twigs outlines the center scene which shows two men walking and a man on horseback. There are tall palm trees in the background and an arabic building topped with a cross.

English, marked as above, Mk. Like 2886, L. V., c 1891

ORIENTAL

made by Petrus Regout

This pattern is very much like Ridgway's "Oriental". The blue is a different shade and is not as intense.

The medallions on the border show a near-eastern temple and a boat, and these alternate with floral patterns.

The center scene is wreathed like Ridgways' and depicts a man on a camel approaching a domed building.

Dutch (Holland), marked P. Regout & Co., L. V., c 1900

ORIENTAL

made by Ridgways

This scalloped edge plate has a border covered in a soft deep blue that is imprinted with little flowers. In the reserves are scenes of a minaret tower and a mosque; these alternate with bouquets. These designs enter the deep well.

The center scene is outlined with a ring of twigs and depicts two men kneeling on a rug and a man standing nearby holding a spear. They are in front of a small temple on a hill at center right. The temple door has an arabic arch. There are tall palm trees at left and in the background are minarets, mountain peaks, and rolling clouds in the sky.

English, marked W. R., Mk. 3316, L. V., c 1891

OYAMA

made by Doulton

This jardiniere has a collar and lower border band of triangular cartouches interspered with scrolls.

The body is printed with a pair of small dragons and one very large dragon; these are Japanese in design.

English, marked Royal Doulton, Mk. 1333, L. V., c 1902

PAGODA

made by William Riagway

The deep saucer shown has sixteen panels and its outer edge is detailed with fishnet pattern. The rim is printed with alternating flowers and sprigs.

The center scene has three Chinese-type buildings. A tall flowering tree rises from center front and in the foreground there are fences and a large overscaled flower.

This backstamp is printed in gothic letters and is difficult to decipher. It seems to read "PESANK". The plate was acquired as "Three Pagodas".

English, marked W. R., Mk. 3301, c 1834

PA JONG

made by Petrus Regout

The bowl shown has an inside border design that alternates three scenic cartouches, showing a boat on an oriental coastline, with three reserves that contain a foliated scroll design; these are joined by small stylized flowers set on a fishscale background. The well is defined by a thin band of scrolls.

The center picture shows a Chinese man and woman on a porch; she is seated on the floor and is holding a parasol, he stands beside her and is balancing the sunshade with one hand. There is a vase at right; a willow tree is in the background, and mountains rise in the distance.

Dutch, Sphinx mark, L. V., c 1900

PEKIN

made by Albert Jones & Co.

The edge of this scalloped plate is printed with various oriental motifs, with scrolls containing fishscales, and cloud designs; small stylized flowers are placed around the rim.

The well is defined by a ring of alternating ovals, half floral, half cross-hatched.

The center design is an arrangement of overscaled peonies set in an urn that is placed on a low footed table.

English. Reg. #538202, marked A. Jones, c 1908

PEKIN

made by Thomas Dimmock

This plate is very slightly scalloped and has 10 panels. The upper half of the rim is covered with a very dark ¾" band of diaper pattern consisting of little diamonds that enclose a circle and a dot. A row of picketting borders the edging. The deep well is defined by a ¾" circle of the same diaper design, but oval reserves are placed in three places in this band and in each there is a scroll pattern. This is also edged with pickets.

The center medallion is composed of a circle of the same pattern as above and this encloses a stylized floral snow-flake type design.

English, marked D, Mk. 1299, E. V., c 1845

PEKIN

made by Authur J. Wilkinson

The rim of this plate is printed in dark cobalt, and with formalized lotus blossoms that alternate with small flowers; these are all encased in a baroque border.

The center scene shows a man with a parasol and a bucket standing in a fenced area. On the ground in front of him is a swan, and a large overscaled flower is in an urn at the right.

English, marked Royal Staffordshire Pottery, Mk. 4170, L. V., c 1909

PEKING

made by Podmore, Walker & Co.

This saucer is paneled with twelve large panels that are formed to round off in scallops at the top edge. The rim is decorated with alternating designs composed of scrolls which enclose fine treillage. These are linked by a small geometric design that encloses an X cross.

The center scene depicts a couple; the woman is seated in a rattan chair with a tall curved back. She is balancing a long-handled parasol, a small dog is seated on the ground beside her. The pig-tailed man stands at left facing the woman. He is carrying a basket in one hand and carries his peaked hat in the other. There is a junk in the harbour behind him, and an over scaled flower is placed in the foreground.

English, marked P. W. & Co., and imp "Pearl Stone Ware", Mk. 3075, E. V., c 1850

PELEW
made by E. Challinor

This paneled plate has fourteen sides and its rim is outlined with a plain dark band. The border has a pattern of flowers that are overlaid with dark leaf-like strokes. The rim of the well is defined by a ½" border of crosshatching and stylized floral oval medallions.

In the left part of the center scene there is a large towered pavilion, the usual tall palm trees, and a bridge that crosses to an island at right. Two other islands are pictured in the background and a little boat flying a pennant is at upper right center.

The Pelew islands are situated 350 miles east of the Phillipines. There are about 75 islands, wooded, mountainous and surrounded by coral reefs.

English, marked E. C., "Ironstone", Mk. 855A, E. V., c 1840

PENANG
made by W. Ridgway

The soup plate photographed has 16 sides and is paneled. The outer edge is printed with a narrow band of zig-zags and oval floral medallions. The rim is printed with large peonies and leaves, and little scenes of a gnarled tree and rock symbols. The well is outlined with a band of circular patterned brocade and oval floral medallions.

The center scene is of many small islands; three have little houses; each is a different shape. At extreme right foreground a man is fishing from the bank, and another man is crossing an arched bridge.

Penang is an island off the Malay Peninsula. (It is also the name of a state and a city there.)

This exact pattern was issued by this same potter, but with the name "Formosa" and with a differently designed back stamp.

English, marked as above, Mk. 3300, E. V., c 1840

RHODA GARDENS

made by Hackwood

This sixteen paneled deep saucer has an edge printed with a gothic type border of scrolls and cartouches ending in trefoils. The rim is printed with four bouquets of dahlias and prunus blossoms descending from the scroll edging.

The well is set off by a ring of chained bricks. The center scene depicts a towered teahouse at right. In front of it are the usual overscaled flowers, and in center front there is a railing. A tall wisteria tree rises in the center, and at left distance are towers, bridges, mountains, water, and a little sailboat.

English, marked "H", Mk. 1860, E. V., c 1850

ROCK

made by Challinor

A very heavy printing of overscaled peonies covers the border of this fourteen sided paneled plate. These are separated by a geometric slanting fence-like design.

The well is defined by a thick ring of floral brocade. The central design is characterized by a dark double square design set on the diagonal, one within and above the other, in the lower right center, from which grows an overscaled peony and a prunus branch which rises to encircle the pattern to the left. At right, and in the distance are towered temples and fences.

English, marked E. C., Mk. 835, E. V., c 1850

SCINDE

made by J. & G. Alcock

The plate is very gently scalloped and is slightly paneled. The rim is outlined with scrolls enclosing a diaper pattern. The border is printed with three groups of stylized dahlias separated by branches of prunus blossoms.

The center scene is dominated by a figure at a little left of center wearing a hat and tunic, pantaloons, and hose. He is carrying a large spotted banner over his shoulder. He is on some steps leading to a small pavilion at left. The tops of palm trees can be seen behind the pavilion. At right rear, there is an ornamental structure on a platform. The foreground contains a lake and rocks and a tall flowering prunus tree that grows through an arch and two very large lotuses at the center. On the reverse side of the plate are sprays of prunus. Note that the cup plates and sauce dishes in Scinde show only the large lotus blossom and structures without the man.

English, marked "Oriental Stone, J. & G. Alcock", Mk. 69, E. V., c 1840

SCINDE

made by Thomas Walker

Scinde is a spelling corruption of the word Sind (or Sindh) which is a province of Pakistan.

The gothic border on this saucer is printed with scrolls that contain grapes, grape leaves and tendrils.

The center scene shows a small teahouse at left; this is connected by a path and terrace steps to a tall pagoda at right center rear. A tall many branched willow rises in the center. In the distance there is a tiny boat on a lake, and at the far distance left there is an island.

English, marked T. Walker, Mk. 3982, E. V., c 1847

SEGAPORE

made by G. Phillips

The saucer photographed has a paneled rim with eighteen narrow panels. Its border pattern covers the rim and consists of shaggy five-petaled flowers and leaves that are printed in a greyish blue, and set against a dark background. The well is defined by a circle of picket design.

The center scene is not truly oriental although the name of the pattern was probably meant to mean Singapore. At first glance the scene looks Swiss. It is a picture of a temple on a lake shore. The roof of the building is upturned slightly at the corners. There are towers behind it, and a small square edifice sits at water level at the left. In the foreground there is a railing with a vase on it, and at the right there are tall trees. The name of the pattern may be Begapore.

English, marked as above with Longport, Mk. 3012, E. V., dated Sept. 3, 1846

SHANGHAE

made by J. Furnival

This fourteen sided paneled plate has a border printed with formalized lotus alternating with prunus floral patterns, and an edging of vertical shaded lines contained within scrolls.

The center design shows a towered teahouse in the left middle distance, a flight of stairs leads downward from the house to a platform. At right center are stylized rocks, big tall leaves and a flowering tree that rises up to curve over the top center. In the foreground are large flowers. In the distance, and beyond a lake, one can see other small houses; there is a boat on the lake, a flag is flying from its rear deck, and two little figures appear in it.

English, marked J. F. & Co., "Ironstone", Mk. 1643, M. V., c 1860

SHANGHAI

made by W. & E. Corn

The edge of this plate is gently scalloped and its rim is covered with contrasting light and dark blue printings of flowers, leaves and small cartouches. This pattern extends into the well. The center scene is of pagodas with upturned roofs set on both sides of a river. A tall flowering tree rises from the left bank to tower in the center of the picture.

English, marked◇W◇, L.V., c 1900

SHANGHAI

made by W. & T. Adams

The edge of this plate is outlined with a triangle diaper pattern, and its border is printed with scenes of a house and a large flowers, these are separated by a cartouche that contains treillage and a stylized lotus.

The well is defined by a circle of honeycomb pattern, and the center scene is composed of many small islands connected by bridges, each island has a tower or pagoda.

In the foreground at right is a large house with many roofs. A bridge crosses from this house to an island at left on which there is a tall tree. On the bridge there are two people, the taller one carries a pole and is followed by the smaller who appears to be a child.

This same pattern originated with Adams in 1818 and was issued in Flow Blue as "Tonquin."

English, marked as above, Mk. 43, M. V., c 1870

SHAPOO:
made by Thomas Hughes

This plate has twelve sides and is paneled. The edge of the rim is outlined by a diamond diaper pattern that alternates with quatrefoils set in reserves formed by scrolls. The border is printed with four large mauresque (Moorish in style and design) cartouches that are filled by a diaper pattern of quatrefoils. These alternate with four large stylized flowers. The pointed bottoms of the cartouches enter the well and are bound together with a ring of criss-cross lines to form a circle around the well.

The center scene shows two musicians on a bridge. One blows an upcurved horn, and the other is playing a long thin horn. At left is an overscaled flower tree. At right a flight of stairs leads upwards from the bridge toward a towered pavilion from which a pennant flies. A tall palm tree rises in the center of the design and in the far distance is an island with a house and trees.

English, marked T.H., Mk. 2121, M. V., c 1860

SIMLA
made by Elsmore & Forster

The border is in this pattern is a design of four scrolled geometric medallions, that alternate with bouquets of dahlia-like flowers. The bottoms of both elements enter the well. The edge is embossed with a circular line and twelve leaves.

The center scene is of a towered pavilion at left. On its porch there stands a man holding a bird net. At right there are tall bamboo trees and the usual overscaled flowers. In the center foreground are two birds with long curving tail feathers. Another plate in this pattern was marked "T. W." Could be Thomas Walker who worked at Tunstall, and who died in 1853. Elsmore & Walker were at Tunstall 1853-1871 and may have acquired this pattern at the time of Walker's death.

English, marked (as above), Mk. 1476, M. V., c 1860

SIVA

maker unknown

The plate shown is printed in many colours. Its border is decorated with alternate panels of coloured flowers on a pale blue background and black flowers on a dark blue striated ground.

The center design is of various coloured large flowers and green and black leaves. Yellow paint has been used over the printing to outline details.

SOBRAON

maker unknown

Plate shown has twelve sides, is paneled, and its rim is outlined by diamond diapering. The border design consists of peony-like flowers and leaves that alternate with six arabesque cartouches. The floral designs enter the well.

The central scene depicts a man on a bridge. He is holding a pennant. At left are two buildings, one is a tower. In the foreground there is a porch-like construction and at the right there is a monument. Overscaled peonies are placed in the foreground, and a tall flowering tree is placed to lean over the center bridge scene.

Sobraon is a village in the Lahore district of India.

This plate has no maker's name or initial. There are prunus blossoms printed on the reverse and just the pattern name.

English, (probably), E. V., c 1850

TAIWAN

made by Joseph Clementson

The sugar bowl photographed has a border design of scrolls that resemble rams' horns. These altnernate with reserves in which there is a little scene of pagodas.

The picture on the body of the vessel is of a pavilion at right center, a fence leads further to the right, under a willow tree, to a larger building. In the foreground there are two standing figures in long robes. They are standing on the banks of a stream and across the water from them is an island with a tall tower and willow trees. This backstamp is difficult to decipher, the name given is a guess.

English, marked J. Clementson, mark 910a (with a Phoenix bird), M. C. c 1850

NOTE: The name Taiwan is incorrect. This pattern is Chusan.

TEMPLE

made by British Anchor Pottery Co., Ltd.

The border of this plate is printed with foliated lambrequins and overscaled dahlias. The center design shows a building at left with an upturned roof. At right middle distance there is another building. A tall tree is placed to fill in the upper circular design and the usual overscaled flowers are in the foreground.

This plate has been painted, over the blue underglaze transfer pattern, with soft dark reds and golds.

English, marked as above, Mk. 624, L. V., c 1910

TEMPLE (THE)

made by Podmore Walker

This plate has a gently scalloped edge that is outlined in very dark blue. Four arabesque forms alternate with four scenes of a temple and flowers around the rim. The deep well is encircled by a ¾ inch brocaded ring of scrolls and triangles.

The center scene is dominated by a large urn at front center left. There is a towered temple at the right, and a little figure with a parasol is on the temple porch. There are other buildings in the background beyond a lake, and a small boat is seen in the middle distance.

English, marked "Pearl Stoneware" P. W. & Co., Mk. 3080, E. V., c 1850

TIMOR

made by Petrus Regout

The border is printed with four large reserves filled with a half of a flower and a diaper patten of circles. Alternating with these are stylized flowers.

The center scene shows two figures, one is a lady standing in a garden, the other seems to be jumping from a roof top nearby and holding onto some tree branches as he falls. In the far distance at right is a tall pointed pavilion from which a pennant is flying.

Timor is an island in the East Indies; the Dutch arrived there shortly after 1613 in search of trade.

Dutch, marked Maastricht, M. V., c 1875 and marked as above.

TOKIO

made by F. Mehlem

The unevenly scalloped plate photographed has a brownish gold lustred edge, and also has shell and scallop embossing around the rim.

The pattern is printed in a greyish blue and covers the entire dish. The background is of stylized flowers and stems and leaves set over a scrollwork pattern. Set into this are four small reserves with Japanese scenes, and one large oval reserve in the center that depicts part of a tree and its branches.

German, marked "F. M.", "Royal Bonn", Thorn pg. 27 Mks. 7 and 8, L. V., c 1891

TONQUIN

made by W. Adams & Son

This fourteen sided paneled plate has a border with a triangular cartouche form alternating with a stylized flower. The central scene has a geometric border. The center design is of many small houses and a tall temple linked by a bridge. On the bridge are two figures at left – one is carrying a lantern suspended from a pole and is closely followed by a small figure in a tunic and dotted skirt, probably a girl. This could relate to the willow legend and the escape of the lovers to their island cottage.

In 1870 this exact pattern was re-issued by Adams and called Shanghai.

English, marked as above, Mk. 22, E. V., c 1845

TONQUIN

made by Joseph Heath

The edge of this twelve sided paneled plate is defined by a narrow band of diamond diapering. The border design is composed of large peonies alternating with three cartouche forms.

The well is detailed with a circular band of diamond designs alternating with floral panels. The center scene shows two men in a fairly large boat, one is fishing, the other guides the tiller.

There is a fence-like structure in the foreground, a tall tree rises from the right bank and the usual overscaled flower is at extreme right. In the distance are two small islands. On the reverse side are sprays of prunus.

The Tonquin region is now North Vietnam. The Gulf of Tonquin lies byeond Hainan Island from Hong Kong, and the city of Tonquin is now Hanoi.

English, marked J. Heath, Mk. 1993, E. V., c 1850

TONQUIN

made by John Meir & Son

The hot plate shown has pierced handles for easy carrying. It is paneled in six large divisions around the rim. A narrow floral diaper pattern surrounds the edge.

The center scene is of a table, at left, on which are some peonies. At right is a tall curving lotus blossom tree. At front center there is scrollwork that serves as a decorative base for the above designs.

English, marked as above, Mk. 2636, M. V., c 1860

TRIPOD
made by Brown, Westwood & Moore
The border of this plate is printed in two different oval cartouches, one double the size of the other, and the edge is gently and unvenly scalloped.

The center scene is dominated by a three-legged stand (a tripod) on which there is placed a tall urn with a lid. The usual overscaled flowers and prunus complete the design.

English, marked "Cauldon," mark on pg. 248 Kovel, L. V., c 1891

WHAMPOA
made by Mellor and Venables
This fourteen sided paneled dish has a deep well. Its outer border is printed in a fish scale pattern contained within scrolls. Small flowers and sprigs are placed within the apertures left by the scroll pattern, but the entire border pattern only covers the top half of the rim.

In this pattern the center design comes up from the well and invades the lower rim. This design features a large towered gate in the front center, with a fancy lantern topped fence at left. A bridge goes over the water to another open edifice at right center in the middle ground. At the upper right is a large high-prowed sail boat with a pennant, and a man is seated at its rear. There are other islands at left and in the far distance. A tall flowering willow tree rises from the middle of the design, and spreads over the top of the entire pattern.

Whampoa was the harbour where boats in the China trade had to tie up and stay in order to do business in Hong Kong.

This example is marked "Ironstone" Imp. in a half circle.

English, marked as noted, see Mk. 2646, E. V., c 1840

WILLOW
made by Doulton & Co.

The bowl photographed is covered on the outside with pictures of the Willow legend; the father's fine house, the willow tree and the peach tree, three figures crossing a bridge, and the pair of doves flying high above the scene. This is a highly stylized version, with the elements of rocks, apple trees, et al, in abstract forms.

English, marked as above, with "Burslem", Mk. 1332, L. V., c 1891

WINDSOR ROYAL
made by James Edwards & Son

This gently scalloped plate has a gilded edge, and a ½ inch deep border of diamond pattern. Stylized flat-petaled prunus and buds are placed around the rim. The well is defined by a circle of beehive designs interspersed with floral reserves.

The center design is a circular grouping of dahlias, buds, stems and leaves.

English, marked "Edwards & Son," Burslem, L. V., c 1880

YEDDO
made by Arthur Wilkinson

The rim of this plate is gently scalloped and is gilded, and there is tiny festoon embossing on the dark printed outer edge. The border shows alternating bouquets with leaves, and a scene of a little towered teahouse. There is some gold placed over the pattern.

The central well is outlined with a little band of triangular forms and floral reserves. At the left, in the center design, is a pagoda with three tiered roofs. A fence is placed in front of this. In the foreground are the usual overscaled flowers and a tall flowering tree is at the right center. Yeddo, like Jeddo, was probably a mispronunciation name for "Tokio."

English, marked Royal Staffordshire, Mk. 4170, L. V., c 1907

No pictures available

CALCUTTA

made by E. Challinor

English, E. V., c 1845

CHAING

made by James Gildea

This is a word that meant "Chinese." The pattern is reported as having been made by the potter above and also by Edge Malkin, and both date c 1885 – 1895

English, marked J. G., see Godden pg. 273, L. V., c 1885

COREA

maker unknown

A platter was described as oriental and bearing only a butterfly as a back stamp.

JARVA

mark not determined

The border on this design is composed of triangular cartouche forms that alternate with a design that terminates in five thin sprays that give a rake effect.

The central design shows a two-storied pagoda at left with trees around it, and at the right a railing on which there are two urns. There are palm trees in the background.

(This information was garnered by looking at a very small and indistinct photograph, and part of the details are undoubtedly missing from the description.)

KREMLIN

made by Samuel Alcock & Co.

A plate observed had a typical oriental type border of stylized geometric designs and flowers.

The center scene shows a small seated figure holding a parasol, and a standing figure to the left.

English, marked S. A. & Co., Mk. 75, E F., c 1840

Scenic Category

AUTHOR'S COLLECTION

ABBEY

made by George Jones & Sons

The cake plate photographed has embossing at the side handles and its edge is outlined with printed scrolls. The border is printed with large cartouches that enclose a scene of Gothic ruins. These are separated by reserves filled with fishnet lines. The bottoms of both these elements join to form a scrolled circle around the well.

The center scene is of a church ruin that has a space for a rose window. In the center ground are larger Gothic ruins.

Not all of the Abbey pattern pieces flow, but some certainly do. This identical pattern was made by Petrus Regout Co. in Maastich, Holland, and the same name was used.

English, marked as above and "1790"
L.V., c 1900

AGRA

made by F. Winkle & Co.

The rim of this platter is outlined with a narrow ½" row of shell design. The border pattern consists of stylized asters and other large blossoms whose leaves are heavily printed in six dividing spots.

The center scene has nothing to do with Agra which is in India, but pictures a Swiss scene with lake, chalet, church with tower, trees and mountains.

English, marked as above, Mk. 4212,
L.V., c. 1891

ANCIENT RUINS

made by Ashworth Bros.

The plate photographed is unevenly scalloped and there is a narrow floral border on the outer edge. The rim is printed with a design of towers and overscaled flowers. The well is encircled by a wreath of leaves and buds.

The center scene shows towers and arches in ruins at the left and an arch and a tall tree at the right. In the center middleground there are a cow and a calf, and in the foreground there are flowers and fallen broken columns. In the distance fields and trees appear.

English, marked imp. "Real Ironstone China", like Mk. 148, L. V., c 1891. Made first by Mason.

ARABESQUE

made by T.J. and J. Mayer

The fourteen sided paneled plate photographed has a rim printed very heavily with curvilinear motifs that are somewhat Moorish in design. These extend into the deep well and give a pointed lace effect.

The scene in the center is European and shows a large chalet with fancy turreted roof. It is enclosed by a stone fence and is situated on the left bank of a stream. There is a tall tree at the right, a grassy bank in the foreground, and a minaret in the distance.

English, marked as above and "Chinese Porcelain," "Longport," Mk. 2570, E.V., c 1845

ATHENS

made by Charles Meigh

This twelve sided paneled plate has a dark printed band around the edge, and a border covered with six large leafy crest-like reserves that alternate with six leaf and scroll patterns.

The center scene depicts an European type ruin and arches set on the bank of a lake. A balustrade extends from this and terminates in a pedestal on which there is a vase. At right foreground there is a terrace and a large covered urn, a tall tree rises at the left.

English, marked C.M., Mk. 2618 or 2614A, E.V., c 1840

AVON (WARE)

made by Booths

This plate is unevenly scalloped and has both bead and scallop embossing. The entire plate is covered with a country scene of meadows, trees and a stream. There are lilies and reeds in the foreground, and in the distance are towers and buildings.

The name "Avon Ware" appears on later china made by the Avon Art Pottery Co. This plate dates about 1880 and was probably made by T. G. & F. Booth before they became Booths Ltd. in 1891.

English, marked as above, L.V., c 1880

COBURG

made by John Edwards

(2 pictures)

The plates in this pattern are twelve sided and are paneled. The border is a Gothic design of quatrefoils connecting grape leaves, grapes and large leafy scrolls. The deep well contains a picture of two men, one with a pole on the bank of a river. In the left background there is a large turreted abbey. At right there is a tall tree and in right distance there is a fortress with a tower. A sailboat is in the middle background. This scene is reversed on the waste bowl shown and three persons appear on the bank.

English, marked J.E., Mk. 1449, E.V., c 1860

COLUMBIA

made by Clementson & Young

The collar of this pitcher is outlined with scrolls on an almost black background. The scrolls are also placed inside the neck, and the base band bears the same pattern.

At right in the central design is a chalet with ornate roof, Gothic windows, arched doors and a balcony. At left across a stream are tall trees and towered buildings, a bridge crosses the center to link these two areas, and a man carrying a net over his shoulders is crossing the bridge. In the middle distance are other buildings and trees.

This pattern has an eagle on the back stamp and from this and the name, it can be deduced that this pattern was produced for the American market.

English, marked as above, Mk. 911, E.V., c 1846

62

CORELLA

probably made by Barker & Son

The octagonal bowl shown has a border of cartouches containing a picture of an urn in a garden, alternating with a diaper pattern of small circles.

The central picture is dominated by a large statue of a woman holding two infants. There are large urns at the right front. A formal garden with a balustrade and fountain are in the middle distance, and in the background there is a castle set against alpine peaks.

English, marked B. & S., Mk. 256, E.V., c 1855

EXCELSIOR

made by Thomas Fell

This plate has twelve sides and is paneled. The top and the bottom parts of the rim are printed with a geometric diaper pattern. The space between is printed with flowers. The deep well is encircled by a pinking design.

The center scene is of classical ruins and a lake. At left there are tall trees, and a woman, man, and child stand on the bank in the foreground. In the distance are other buildings and mountain peaks.

English, marked T. F. & Co., Mk. 1534,, E.V., c 1850

GENEVA
made by Royal Doulton

The border pattern on this plate is composed of large feathery scrolls and baroque cartouches on a field filled with straight horizontal lines. In each reserve there is a picture of edelweiss.

The central scene is of a Swiss farm house and a mill with a water wheel on a stream. The snowcapped Alps appear behind the mill. At left is a tall leafy tree and in the front center two goats recline on the bank. Two figures stand on a small hill near the water wheel.

The next picture is also of Geneva pattern. The border is the same, but it is printed in a much darker blue. The center scene differs from the first plate shown. It pictures an alpine lake nestled between lulls and mountains. There is a house in the middle ground, at left tall trees on both sides of the scene, and buildings on the lake shore in the distance. The two goats appear at left front and two figures are standing near them.

It is probable that different patterns were placed on different sized dishes in this set. Doulton also did this with their Watteau pattern.

English, marked as above, Mk. 1327, L.V., each is dated 1906, 1907

GENEVESE
made by Edge Malkin

This plate has an unevenly scalloped edge and its border is printed with flowers and baroque leafy scrolls. The well is defined by a circular ribbed band that is fringed on both sides.

The center scene is of a chalet set in a garden. There are overscaled flowers in the foreground, and in the distance there are tall trees and towered buildings.

Note that Clews made a soft paste plate in brown transfer and named it Genevese.

English, marked as above, Mk. 1445, M.V., c 1873

GOTHA

made by Joseph Heath

The plates in this pattern have twelve sides and are slightly paneled. The border is printed with oblong floral designed cartouches, and these alternate with shield forms. Both elements are linked by garlands of curved quillwork that forms a circle around the well.

The central design depicts a chalet with a tower that is situated on a lake. The chalet is elaborately decorated with dormers and crockets and spires, and its windows are diamond paned. At left there is a tall tree, and in the left distance there is a castle. The foreground is composed of grass and small bushes.

Gotha is a city in Thuringia in Germany.

English, marked J.H., could be Mk. 1993, E. V., c 1850

GOTHIC

made by Jacob Furnival

This twelve-sided paneled plate has a border printed heavily with scrolls, grapes, grape leaves, and tendrils. The lower sections of the bunches of grapes enter the well. The central scene shows a large cathedral at left center. It is connected by a stone bridge which crosses a stream in the center, to the right bank where tall trees grow. Two men are fishing from the bridge. In the background there are other abbey-like buildings.

English, marked W. R. & Co., Mk. 1643, E. V., c 1850

GRECIAN

made by Ridgways

The soup plate shown has an unevenly scalloped and gilded edge that is further enhanced by a row of printed beading. The plate is printed in soft blue. Its upper rim is covered with dainty flowers and leaves; there are six small scroll designs evenly spaced at the top edge. A row of chain design separates the upper and lower rims. The latter is decorated with vertical divisions that contain a stem of leaves, these terminate into a wreath of poppies and smaller flowers.

In the center there is a picture of colonnaded temples at the left, in the center there is a river scene with boats, and at right a man and woman standing leaning against a parapet shaded by tall trees.

English, marked as above, Mk. 3316, L.V., c 1893

GRECIAN SCROLL

made by T. J. & J. Mayer

The deep saucer shown has sixteen panels and the border is printed with running scrolls of acanthus leaves and hence the name of the pattern. The well is detailed with a ring of lacy beads and dots.

The central scene is Gothic, and depicts a stone parapet and tall trees in the left foreground, and a chalet and towers in the right middleground and distance.

English, marked as above and "Longport", Mk. 2571, E.V., c 1850

GRECIAN STATUE

made by Brownfields

The outer rim of this scalloped plate is rounded and raised. Its border is printed with six garlanded reserves, three contain a scene of a tower, and three have a picture of some urns. These are connected with floral bouquets. The bottoms of these enter the well and form a wreath.

The center scene is of an equestrian statue of a man in a skirted costume, like a long tunic. The statue is set upon a large rectangular base which is decorated with a scene of Grecian women. In the foreground there are pieces of broken columns and parts of broken statues and some flowers. In the background there is a river with a boat upon it, some trees, and in the distance there are towers.

English, marked as above, Mk. 670, L.V., c 1891

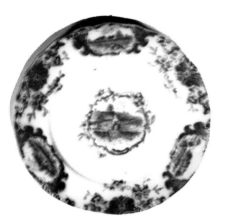

HOMESTEAD

made by J. & S. Meakin

This plate is scallop-edged and has wave and scroll embossing. Its border is printed with three medallions that show a farm house and land; these alternate with three scroll and floral patterns.

The center medallion is wreathed with flower stems and leaves, and depicts a stone water mill.

English, marked as above, Mk. 2602, L.V., c 1907

ITALIA

made by W. & E. Corn

The scalloped edge of this plate sets off a rim printed with treillage (lattice work) over a dark ground. The upper border is printed with a row of morning glories and leaves that twine over a rod. The treillage design enters the well and gives a picket effect.

In the foreground of the center scene a man is fishing from the bank of a stream. A woman stands at the center holding a child by its hand, and carrying a net over her shoulder. The child leads a dog.

In the background there is a sailboat. A bridge crosses the stream at the middle distance. In the far distance there are classical rivers and Tuscany type buildings.

This scene first appeared on "Tivoli" by Furnival (c 1845) and appears on a later plate issued by J. Kent in 1910 and named "Oriental."

English, marked W L.V., c 1891

JEDDO

made by W. Adams & Co.

This scalloped edge bowl has 4 inch deep shell-like embossing. The rim is outlined with a ¾" printed border of flowers and leaves. Bouquets of flowers alternate with sprays of large leaves around the rim.

The center scene is encircled with a chain-like design, and shows a pastoral scene of two shepherds and a cow in the foreground, and tall trees and Romanesque ruins in the background.

English, marked as above, like Mk. 2831, L.V., c 1893

JENNY LIND

made by Arthur Wilkinson Ltd.

This is not a portrait plate although it undoubtedly honored the great Swedish singer who became a British subject in 1859 at the age of 39, and died there in 1887, after a lifetime career leading to international honor.

The design is simple, and has no border trim. Almost the entire dish is covered with a scene showing five people in Mid-Victorian dress at the left. They are standing under a very tall tree and are looking at a scene of boulders, a castle, a lake, and alpine peaks.

English, marked Royal Staffordshire Pottery, Mk. 4170, L.V., c 1895

LEICESTER

made by Sampson Hancock

The platter photographed has a scalloped gilded edge and the border is printed with four reserves depicting hunting and coaching scenes. These alternate with oval medallions that contain a stylized bouquet in an urn. They are joined by a very dark background in which are printed stylized vases with flowers. The well is defined by fringed scallops.

English, marked H. & S., Mk. 1933, L.V., c 1906

LOZERE

made by Edward Challinor

The damaged plate photographed was a gift and the only example available as this book goes to print. The plate has twelve sides and is paneled. The background of the border is composed of continuous straight lines. Shields that are framed by scrolls are placed around the rim, and these alternate with a design of trees and a castle. The center picture is of a formal garden. Two women are in the foreground near a semi-circular stone bench and a cherub-supported fountain. In the background there is a lake, a bridge with arches, and tall trees. In the distance there is a castle with many towers.

English, marked E. Challinor, Mk. 835A, E.V., c 1850

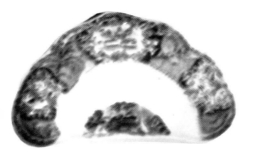

MALTA

made by F. A. Mehlem

The bone dish used for an example of this pattern is printed in a greyish blue and has a scalloped edge. The border design consists of reserves depicting minarets and towers that alternate with floral cartouches. These elements are connected with a blue dotted field. This pattern may not be Flow Blue.

The center scene shows oriental buildings with mosque-like domed roofs.

German, marked "F.A.M. Bonn" Mk. o, pg. 207 Kovel, c 1891

MATTEAN

made by Brownfields Pottery Ltd.

This twelve sided, slightly paneled soup plate has a border of oval medallions that frame a scene of a couple, in court costume, seated beside a birdhouse, in the background there is a castle and mountains.

The well is defined by a picket ring of fleur-de-lis design.

In the foreground of the center picture there appears a couple, the woman is dressed in a full skirted costume and is seated, the man stands next to her and wears a short cape. They are placed on a bridge that is situated over a formal waterfall. In the background there is a castle, a river, and trees and mountains.

English, marked as above with Cobridge. Reg. #555592, Mk. 670, L. V. 1898

NOTE: The name Mattean is incorrect. This pattern is Watteau.

McNETTE

made by J. Dimmock

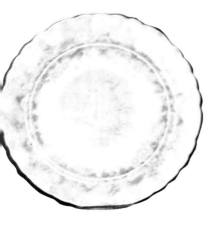

This plate is scalloped and paneled. The border is printed with flowers that enter the well. The center scene is of a Scottish castle and tower in the middle ground, with a tall tree at right and a mountain at far left.

From 1878 the firm of Dimmock was headed by W. D. Cliff and his name appears on the company's marks.

English, marked "Cliff", Mk. 1295, L.V., c 1891

NON PAREIL

made by Burgess & Leigh

The edge of this plate is outlined by ¼ inch border of tiny fleurs-de-lis and is slightly scalloped. The rim design alternates scenes of towered buildings and large baroque scrolls. Poppies are placed between these.

The center scene shows a standing man and a seated woman in the foreground. There are towered buildings and a pine tree at the right rear; there is a lake in the center middle ground, and a tall tree at left. In the left background there are other towered buildings. In the far distance there are alpine peaks and floating clouds.

English, marked B. & L., Mk. 712, L.V., c 1891

OLD CASTLE

made by W. & E. Corn

The plate at hand has a scalloped edge that is outlined with a whitish narrow line. The border is printed on a field of grey blue and the design is of a wreath made of dahlias, peonies, and chrysanthemums with leaves and sprigs; the bottom of these enter the well and form a wreath around it.

The center picture is dominated by a castle with Gothic windows and a tall tower. In the foreground there is some grass and a fenced road on which two men are standing at the left. At right there is a tall feathery tree and in the distance there are trees and a church tower.

This plate has two marks. It is back-stamped W for W. & E. Corn of the Staffordshire potteries, and impressed B. & L. who were also at the Staffordshire Potteries. The guess would be that one potter made the plate and the other decorated it.

English, marked as described, L.V., 1891

ORIENTAL

made by James Kent

This very gently scalloped plaque has an embossed edge that is ¾" deep, and comprises most of the border. This dish was probably meant to be hung and used as a picture. The entire surface is covered by a picture of a family on a fishing expedition. There are sheep near them, sailboats on the water, an arched bridge and a mixture of European buildings. There is a Greek ruin high on a hill in the left background. There is no detail that is oriental in the design, and as a matter of fact this same scene appears on a plate made by W. & E. Corn, named "Italia" which probably ante-dates this plaque, and also on "Tivoli" made by Furnival, c 1845

English, marked J. Kent, Mk. like 2265, L.V., c 1910

RHINE

made by Thomas Dimmock

This plate has a gently scalloped edge and the rim is printed with stylized oak leaves and Gothic arch forms.

The center scene shows a chalet with fanciful roof and Victorian crockets at the left. This is situated on a river and has arches in its basement that are at the water's edge. At the right there are a pine tree and an oak tree. In the middle distance there is a bridge and beyond that a tower.

English, marked T.D. "Kaolinware," Mk. 1298, dated May 7, 1844

RHONE

made by Thomas Furnival;

This old plate has twelve sides and is paneled. The border design consists of Gothic arch patterns alternating with clusters of grapes and leaves.

The center scene, set in the deep well, shows a tall tree at left foreground. An arched bridge crosses a river; two people, one with a pole, stand on the bridge. There are chalet-type buildings at the right, and others appear in the far distance.

English, marked T. F. & Co., Mk. 1645, E. V., c 1845

SHANGHAI

made by W.H. Grindley

The platter shown has an outer border rim of printed beads. Four scenic reserves depict two little figures near buidings. These alternate with cartouche forms enclosing flowers.

The center scene is not Chinese, it is European. At left is a stone fountain, pedestal, and urn. At front center there are two people, a standing man and a child sitting on a parapet. The middle is dominated by a large river or lake, and in the right background are Italianate buildings with towers and mountains.

English, marked as above, Mk. 1842, L.V., c 1891

TIVOLI

made by Thomas Furnival

This twelve sided, slightly paneled plate has a border of stylized small flowers and scrolls interwoven to make a formal design. The edge of this enters the well.

The center scene depicts a pastoral setting on a lake shore. A family group is fishing in the foreground. There are tall trees on the shore, boats on the lake, and towered buildings on a hill at left center rear.

English, marked T. F. & Co. "Real Ironstone," Mk. 1645, E.V., c 1845

TOGO

made by F. Winkle

Small embossed flowers and scrolls encircle the rim of this scalloped plate. The border is printed with flowers and swags.

The center well is defined by a ½" band of fringed dark blue.

The center design is a lake scene with a covered gondola-type boat and sailboats. At left center there is a tall tree and in the background there are many buildings dominated by two tall domed towers.

English, marked as above, Mk. 4215, L.V., c 1900

TROY

made by Charles Meigh

This dish has a gently and unevenly scalloped edge, and its outer border is printed with reverse scallops that terminate in diamond pendants with trefoils. Placed around the rim are six large flowers with buds, leaves and stems. The well is defined by a Gothic design of diamond pendants and trefoils on a scalloped base.

The center scene is European and portrays Gothic ruins with tall trees at the left. In the far distance there are a castle and a church. At right mid-center there is a bridge which crosses to an island. In the foreground are three figures, a man, a woman, and a child in Victorian costume. They are standing on a bank, and the man is pointing to the island.

English, marked C. M., Mk. 2614A and Mk. 2618, E.V., c 1840

TYROLEAN

made by William Ridgway & Co.

This plate has Ridgway's typical scrolled, ribbed, embossed (gadroon) rim. The border is printed with alternating large flowers, rounded design forms, and sprays of edelweiss.

The center scene is of mountain and lake scenery. Two persons are seated (on the grass) in the right foreground; there are two goats behind them. Trees rise on the left, and in the right distance, high on a hill, there are turreted buildings and a church.

English, marked W. R. & Co., Mk. 3303A, E. V., c 1850

VENICE

could be by Bishop & Stonier

This clock is part of a mantel set that consists of a pair of vases and the clock. A typical Victorian Romantic scene of castles, towers, water and trees appear on all these items. The clock shown has the same scene set in medallions at the top and bottom, and again on the main body of the case. The side pillars are embossed.

English, marked B. & S., could be Mk. 384, L.V., c 1891

VERONA

made by Ford & Sons, Ltd.

The edge of this plate is printed with tiny scallops. The border design consists of four reserves which contain scenes of lambs grazing. These are separated by baroque scroll and heart designs. The well is defined by a delicate lacy circle.

English, marked F. & Sons Ltd., Mk. 1586, L.V., c 1908

VIGNETTE

made by J. Dimmock & Co.

The unevenly scalloped edge of this plate is also embossed. The upper border is printed on a soft blue background with pale flowers and sprigs. The lower half of the rim is also printed with flowers and sprigs, but in a deep blue, and this extends into the well.

The center scene shows an old castle with towers. In the foreground there is a grassy knoll on which bushes and flowers grow.

English, marked Cliff, Mk. 1295, L.V., c 1891

 **VISTA**

made by G.L. Ashworth & Bros. Ltd.

The platter photographed has an embossed ridged edge and is scalloped. The upper border is white, and the rest of the rim is printed with large vine leaves and tendrils. The center scene shows some people dressed in Victorian costume, standing on a lawn shaded by tall trees at both right and left. In the foreground there is a balustrade and in the distance stands a large manor house.

This example is blurred on the leaves of the rim, but the rest of the pattern is clear. It may not be Flown.

English, marked Mason's, Mk. 2530, L.V., c 1891

NOTE: This pattern is NOT Flow Blue.

WALMER

could be made by Elijah Hodgkinson

The ten sided plate photographed is paneled and its border is printed with four vignettes showing a couple standing in front of a tent-like building. These are separated by groups of leaves that terminate into garlands of small leaves that form a circle around the well.

The center scene depicts a couple standing in front of a large equestrian statue at right. In the left background there is a castle and a lake, and in the distance are alpine peaks. Walmer is probably a German or Swiss scenic attraction.

English, marked E.H. see Godden pg. 716, M.V., c 1865

WASHINGTON
made by Thomas Walker

This twelve sided paneled dish has a deep line or indentation set just inside its edge, and this further defines the outer rim. The border is printed with five reserves, each containing a picture of Greco-European buildings; these are connected by floral cartouche forms. The well is outlined for ¾" by a fish scale diaper pattern.

The center scene is the usual romanticized European landscape with tall formal buildings at right center, gondolas and boats on a lake, tropical trees, and alpine peaks.

The mark on the backstamp was used only from 1845 – 1851.

English, marked as above, Mk. 3982a, E.V., c 1848

WASHINGTON VASE
made by Podmore & Walker

The border is printed with small medallions in each of which there is a picture of a vase in the foreground, and buildings in the distance. These are separated by scrolled reserves filled with fish net diaper pattern and crowned at the top with flowerets. The well is outlined by a wreath of the same small flowers.

The center picture is dominated by a large covered urn at left. Its handles are made of birds with outstretched wings, and it is decorated with a scene of a running deer. At right is a smaller urn with long straight handles. The usual Victorian romantic scenic elements are present in the background, tall tropical trees, a lake, and castle-like buildings.

English, marked as above, Mk. 3080, E.V., c 1850

WATTEAU

by Davenport

This is a picture of a chop plate. Its border is edged in very dark blue and is unevenly and gently scalloped, and the rim is printed with a scallop shell design that alternates with cartouche forms. These are printed over a fine netted and paisley design. In each cartouche there are garlands of roses.

The central scene depicts a terrace on which stand a man and woman dressed in court costumes. At left a woman sits on a stool under a tree, and man, with a little dog nearby, half reclines on the grass. At right there is a fountain composed of a cherub holding a dolphin water spout. There is a columned classic ruin in the right distance.

English, marked as above, Mk. 1181A, E.V., dated 1844

WATTEAU

by Doulton

This is a later rendition of the Watteau by Davenport. The border design is identical.

The center scene differs on different items in the dinner service produced. But often it is of a lady with a lute. She is seated and a man stands near her at center in a garden. Watteau was a famous French court painter who died in 1721, and his paintings inspired these designs.

In reply to an inquiry, Doulton Fine China Ltd. wrote that this pattern was introduced into their line in 1896 and production ceased in 1930.

Note: A pitcher in this pattern marked H. H. & Co. was inspected. These are the initials of Hales Hancock & Goodwin, who were retailers of china in London from 1922 1960.

English, marked as above, Mk. 1328, L.V., c 1900

WATTEAU

could be made by Charles Meigh

The octagonal platter shown has a border design dominated by four large scenic medallions that depict a castle and a parapet with an urn. These are joined by a diaper pattern of fish net. The well is defined by a border of baroque scrolls.

The center scene shows two standing figures dressed in court clothes and two people seated on the grass at right center. A statuary fountain is at left, and a stairway leads down to a lawn at right. There is the usual Victorian Romantic scenery in the background, a lake, castles and towers, trees and mountains.

Watteau was a painter who depicted the French court life during the reign of Louis XIV. His influence continued long after his death in 1721.

Note similarity to Davenport's Watteau. These potters were contemporaries.

English, impressed mark could be Meigh, E.V., c 1850

WATTEAU

made by New Wharf Pottery

The border on this plate is printed with the identical pattern used by Davenport and Doulton, but the edge is scalloped and deeply embossed with little rounded edges.

The center garden scene has a lady playing a lute, and a man plays a flute.

New Wharf Pottery ceased as such in 1894, so it is reasonable to assume that Doulton took over the pattern in 1896. New Wharf may have obtained the pattern in 1887 when Davenport's closed; the new Wharf Pottery Co. operated from 1878 – 1894, and Doulton obtained the Watteau pattern in 1896.

English, marked NWP Co., Mk. 2883, L.V., c 1891

WILD ROSE

made by George Jones

This is a famous old pattern first p
duced by J. Meir and Son. The exam
shown is not flow blue, but it is stated
established dealers that it was made in f
blue. The border is printed with wild rose
hence the name.

The center scene depicts a village in
background. In right middle ground ther
a barn and a bridge. The foreground
basically a river scene, and men are pun
flat boats in the water.

English, marked "Improved Wild R
964," L.V., c 1910

No pictures available

ACADIA

These plates have scalloped edges. The
border is printed with flowers and the center
medallion has a boat scene.

ATALANTA

made by Wedgwood & Co.

The plates in this pattern have scalloped,
beaded, and gilded edges. The border pattern
is of roses, and the center scene is a romantic
one like Doulton's Watteau.

English, marked as above, Mk. 4057C,
L.V., c 1900

ATHENS

made by Wm. Adams & Son

This plate often appears in light blue, bu
no flow blue has been obtained, although
may have been produced. It is the usua
romantic scenic type of design.

English, marked Ironstone, Mk. 23, E.V.
c 1849

MARCUS

A plate observed at a show bearing th
name had a center scene depicting statue
figures, and trees.

No pictures available

RHONE

made by Wood & Brownfield, c 1845

RHONE SCENERY

made by T. J. & J. Mayer

These plates are paneled and scrolls are rinted around the edge. The border is deep nd consists of paneled linear lines that rcumscribe the center. The rim is divided to five panels, and there is a rose garland in ich panel.

The center scene depicts a chateau and ees at left, and there is a tower in the iddle distance. A sod covered bridge is laced prominently in the foreground, and anding on it are two people with a child ated nearby.

The example used here for descriptive urposes was printed in pale blue, but flow lue could have been made.

English, marked as above, E.V., c 1850

TEMPLE

made by Whittingham, Ford & Co.

The scene on this pattern is of Greco-Roman buildings in a classical landscape. The printing was done in a medium blue.

English, marked W. F. & Co., Mk. 4130, M.V., c 1868

AUTHOR'S COLLECTION

Floral Category

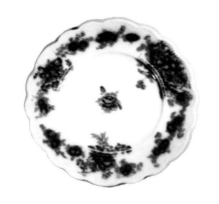

ALBANY

made by W.H. Grindley

This plate has a scalloped, beaded edge further detailed with floral and scrolled embossing. The border is printed with groups of roses, dahlias and for-get-me-nots. The leaves from these bouquets enter the well. The well is detailed with scalloped embossing.

In the center of the well is one full blown rose.

English, marked as above, Mk. 1842, LV., c. 1899

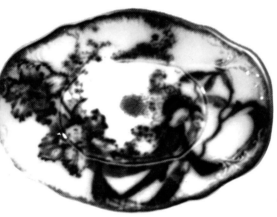

ALEXANDRIA

made by Hollinshead & Kirkhan

The tray photographed has unevenly scalloped edges with fluted embossing and some scroll embossing.

An asymetrical design of large gladioli and little leafy sprigs covers the entire surface. Gold lustre has been placed around the rim and in the center.

English, marked as above, MK. 2073, Reg. #218832, L.V., c. 1900

AMBROSIA

made by Wood & Brownfield

This plate is printed in a medium light blue. It has an unevenly scalloped edge and there is embossing around the rim that forms a heavy ridge and leaf-like scrolls. The scrolls are gilded and there is lustre around the outer edge. The border is printed with bouquets of pink and brown flowers with buds and these are linked by a wreath of willow leaves.

The center design of a small bouquet is encircled by a wreath of the same leaves. There are gilt highlights on the design.

English, marked W. & B., Mk. 4242, E. V., c. 1840

ANEMONE

made by Minton

These plates are gently scalloped and the border is trimmed with stylized anemonies and leaves. Some of the sprigs of leaves enter the well.

The center design is of a pair of anemonies.

English, marked B. B., Mk. 2705, M. V., c. 1860

ANEMONE

made by Bishop & Stonier

The pitcher photographed has a dragon shaped handle. The scales of the dragon are dark blue touched up with gold and the collar at the top is also in very dark blue and is outlined with gold. The body is covered with large drawings of these wild flowers of the spring.

Anemonies are usually five petaled and are usually white. The Greeks gave them their name and it means literally "Daughter of the Wind".

English, marked B. & S., Mk. 384, Reg. 174406, L.V., c. 1891

ARCADIA

made by Authur Wilkinson

This is a very gently scalloped plate with floral and festoon embossing. The rim is printed with baroque scrolls and bouquets of flowers, three in baskets and three loose. Some of the bouquet sprigs enter the well.

The center design is of an urn filled with flowers, and there are two long-tailed, crested birds on branches near the urn.

English, marked Royal Staffordshire Pottery, Mk. 4170, L.V., c. 1907

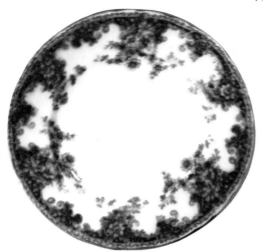

ATHOL

made by Burgess & Leigh

A circle of small scrolls outlines the unevenly scalloped and gilded edge of this plate. The border is printed with asters and leaves that are placed in baroque scroll reserves. These alternate with a design of foliated scrolls. Some of the sprays of flowers enter the well.

English, marked as above, Mk. 718, Reg. #324171, L.V., c. 1910

AUROREA

made by Petrus Regout

The border of this plate is printed with leafy scrolls and bell-like flowers that twine around a circular ring.

The center design is of roses and leaves and buds all on a single stalk. This design fills the well.

Dutch, marked P.R., M.V., c. 1867

AYR

made by W. & E. Corn

This is a heavy plate, embossed with scrolls around the edge. The rim is printed with baroque semi-cartouches that alternate with groups of little flowers. The sprigs from these enter the well.

Ayr is the name of a county in Scotland.

English, marked as above, Mk. 1113, L.V., c. 1900

BATH

made by Robert Heron & Son

Baroque scrolls filled with little flowers swirl around the rim which is gilt edged. Three groups of large flowers alternate with three groups of small flowers. All of the larger groups are in the well. Leaves, flowerets, and sprigs from the smaller groups also enter the well.

Scotland, marked as above, Mk. 2014, M.V., c. 1870

BEATRICE

made by J. Maddock & Son

This plate is printed in a silver blue. The edge is unevenly scalloped and is gilded. A single line of embossing also outlines the edge. There is garland embossing draped over the rim. The upper rim is printed with a wreath of forget-me-nots, and the lower border has a design of pansies and forget-me-nots, sprays of the latter enter the well and are set upon a chain of diamonds and scroll links.

English, marked as above, Mk. 2469, L.V. c. 1896

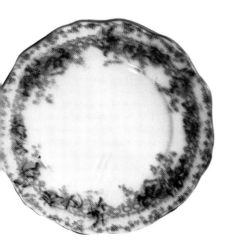

BENTICK

made by Cauldon

The backstamp on this plate is a crown and belt, an old Ridgway mark used by Cauldon in the early 1900's. Cauldon bought Brown, Westhead and Moore, who succeeded Bates, Brown, Westhead and Moore, who had purchased Ridgway & Bates. This backstamp is initialed JR; standing for J. Ridgway who first produced this design in c 1850. See Godden Mk. 3257.

The pattern on this scalloped edge plate is of oriental florals printed on the border. The well is defined by a ring of flowers and brocade pattern.

The center is a mass of swirling circles of dahlias, leaves and leafy foliage.

This exact mark with the name "Bentick" can be seen in Godden's Handbook, P. 112.

English, marked JR, Mk. 822, L.V., c. 1905

BLOSSOM

made by G.L. Ashworth & Bros.

The border design on this plate is of wild roses and leaves. The rim is outlined with a circle of thorny stems.

The center design shows a nosegay of two wild roses and leaves.

English, marked "Real Ironstone China", Mk. 139, M.V., c. 1865

BLUE ROSE

made by W.H. Grindley

This plate has a very deep cobalt border. The edge is scalloped and beaded and embossed with little flowers. A gold tracing of vine leaves is placed over the rim. The well is defined by scallop embossing.

One large full blown rose is in the center of the plate.

This pattern is exactly like "Trent" by Wood & Sons.

English, marked as above, Mk. 1842, L.V., c. 1900

BOUQUET

made by Henry Alcock

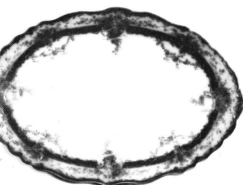

This set of dishes has scalloped edges outlined with gold and embossing. Scroll embossing encircles the border. There are three large groups of daisy-like flowers alternating with three smaller floral motifs on the rim and these are connected by a 3/8" border of dark blue over printed with scrolls. Tiny sprays and floral garlands enter the center well.

English, marked as above, Mk. 65, L.V., c. 1895

BOUQUET

maker unknown

These twelve sided plates are paneled. The rim is outlined by a fleur-de-lis and cable design. The border is printed with three large flower arrangements that alternate with single flowers. Each of these is a different flower. The deep well is penetrated by the bottoms of the border design.

The center picture is of a bouquet of morning glories and dahlias, large leaves and small sprays.

English, marked F. & W., Mk. 4435, E.V., c. 1850

BRAMBLE

made by Alfred Meakin

The gently scalloped border of this plate is covered with blackberries, blackberry vine tendrils, leaves and little blossoms. The leaves and flowers are gilded.

English, marked as above, Mk. 2583, L.V.V, c. 1891

BRIGHTON

made by Ridgways

The very gently scalloped edge on this plate is gilded. For-get-me-nots are printed in a fairly light blue with stems and leaves in a darker blue. They are placed in a circling arrangement around the rim. There is some gold on the stems.

English, marked as above, Mk. 3310, L.V., c. 1910

BRUNSWICK

made by Wood & Sons

The plate has a slightly scalloped rim with tiny floral embossing around the edge. The rim is printed in very dark blue and depicts branches of five petaled dogwood-like flowers. Some of these enter the well.

English, marked Royal Semi-Porcelain, Mk. 4285, L.V., c. 1891

CAMBRIDGE

made by New Wharf Pottery

This plate has a scalloped edge, and an embossed line, connected with shell forms, which encircle the rim. The plate is divided into three large patterns of ruffled peonies placed on a very dark and baroque background. The leaves of the peonies are printed over this in a blackish-blue.

The center design is one full peony bloom and stem.

English, marked as above, Mk. 2886, L.V., c. 1891

CATHERINE

made by W.H. Grindley

The unevenly scalloped gilded edge of this plate has comb-like embossing around the rim. Sprays of rose-like flowers are printed all around the border, and in a few places the sprays enter the well.

English, marked as above, Mk. 1842, Reg. #233436, L.V., c. 1891

CECIL

made by F. Till & Son

The scalloped edge of this plate is outlined by scroll embossing. The border is printed with a dark edge in which appear small flowers. The plate is divided into six panels by pillar like designs. Enclosed in each is a multi-flowered branch.

English, marked as above, Mk. 3857, L.V., c. 1891

CEICEL

made by Upper Hanley Pottery

This plate has a gently scalloped edge. The border is printed with ten cartouches, each containing the same bouquet of small flowers.

The center design is a bouquet of single petaled flowers, and sprays, and a basket form is indicated by scrolls and treillage.

English, marked as above, Mk. 3929A, L.V., c. 1891

CHATSWORTH

made by Sampson Hancock

The square vegetable bowl photographed has a gilded edge and vertical embossing in the corners. It is printed asymetrically with bouquet of poppies and daisies on one side and single blossoms on the opposite side.

English, marked as above, Mk. 1932, L.V., c. 1906

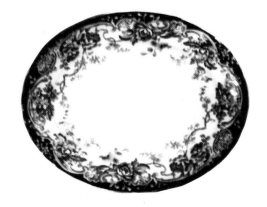

CHATSWORTH

made by Keeling & Co.

The platter photographed has a dark greyish blue printing on a scalloped form. The border strip is very dark and is over printed with flower buds. Baroque scrolls and large flowers alternate with sprays and leaves on the rim. The tendrils from the sprays enter the well.

English, marked as above, Mk. 2243, L.V., c. 1886

CHRYSANTHEMUM

made by Myott, Son & Co.

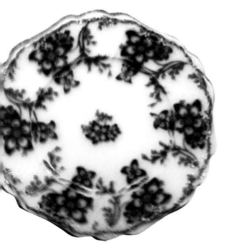

The sponge dish shown has a rim edging of an elongated fleur-de-lis. The pattern on the lid is of light greyish-blue chrysanthemums and leaves, and gold lustre is dusted over this. The handle is gold touched and a gilt border encircles the lid.

The basin is also printed with the chrysanthemums.

English, marked as above, Mk. 2911, L.V., c. 1907

CLAREMONT

made by Johnson Bros.

This six sided plate has a scalloped embossed edge. Stylized flowers and stems are placed at six spots around the rim and these are connected by sprigged stems. Flowers and stems both enter the well.

The center design shows two little flowers and stems.

English, marked as above, Mk. 2177, L.V., c. 1891

CLAREMONT GROUPS

made by Sampson Hancock

The soup plate photographed has a slightly scalloped rim outlined with a printed sawtooth trim. Three large sprays of realistic flowers alternate with three single flowers with stem and leaves. All the flowers are of different variety from each other.

The center has a single daisy type flower.

English, marked S.H., Mk. 1927, M.V., c. 1860

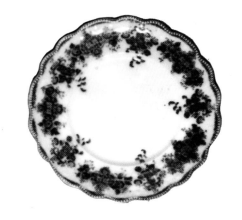

CLARENCE

made by W.H. Grindley

The rim of this plate is scalloped and beaded and a row of tiny embossed flowers is set inside the beading. The pattern on the border consists of baroque cartouches flanked by flowers, alternating with small bouquets from which tendrils extend into the well. The well is outlined with small lace-like embossing.

English, marked as above, Mk. 1842, L.V., c. 1900

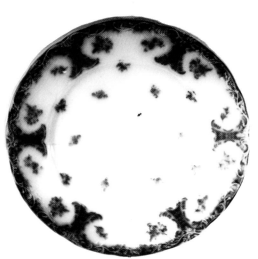

CLARISSA

made by Johnson Bros.

The scalloped edge of this plate is outlined by floral and wave embossing. The border is printed in six places with a curved vertical oblong design outlined with small feathers. The entire plate, rim and well, is sprigged with small flowers.

English, marked as above, Mk. 2177, L.V., c. 1900

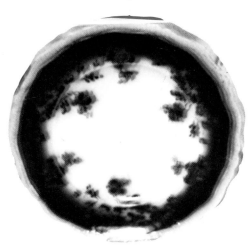

CLAYTON

made by Johnson Bros.

This plate has a scalloped gilt edge which is embossed ½" deep over a white border. The rest of the rim is covered with cobalt blue over which are printed small petunias. Sprigs and buds from these enter the well.

English, marked as above, Mk. 2177, L.V., c. 1902

CLEVEDON

made by Ridgways

The gravy boat pictured has a scalloped edge. There is some embossing around the top and on the handle. The border is printed with wild roses and buds, leaves and sprigs.

English, marked as above, Mk. 3312, L.V., c. 1905

CLYDE

made by New Wharf Pottery

The scalloped edge of this plate is set off with scroll and shell embossing. Gold is placed on the scrolls. The border is printed with three garlands of jonquils, and these alternate with bouquets of lilies and petaled flowers. The patterns are joined by scrolls and tips of the flowers enter the well.

The center design is a three flower bouquet with leaves.

English, marked as above, Mk. 2886, L.V., c. 1891

COBURG

made by Thos. Dimmock

The unevenly scalloped edge of this plate is outlined with a diaper pattern set on very dark blue, set within baroque scrolls. The plate has a deep well and is printed with three large groups of flowers, each different. Alternating with these, and also in the center, are small sprigs.

English, marked T.D., "Stone Ware", Mk. 1299, E.V., c. 1845

CORA

made by J. Kent

This plate has a scalloped edge with a raised fluted embossing with gilt trim. The border design is of four large cartouches that contain flowers and are separated by scallop shells.

The center design is a bouquet of flowers and sprigs.

English, marked as above, Mk. 2264, L.V., c. 1891

NOTE: The name of this pattern may be Dora.

CRETE

made by J.R. Plant & Co.

This plate has a scalloped edge that is trimmed with gold. The outer border is very dark, almost black, and dotted with gold. The border pattern consists of sprays of wild roses, peonies, and smaller flowers and leaves. Some of the small flowers enter the well.

English, marked Stoke Pottery, Mk. 3056, L.V., c. 1889

DAHLIA

made by Upper Hanley

This plate has a scalloped, embossed and gilded edge. Its rim is divided into three large floral groups by shell motif embossing and shell printing.

The center picture is of a large bouquet of dahlias.

English, marked as above, Mk. 3928, L.V., c. 1895

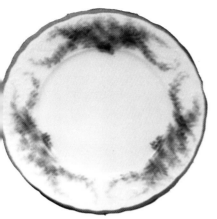

DAISY

made by Burgess & Leigh

This plate has a gently scalloped gilded edge with feather embossing, and some scroll embossing. Bouquets of daisies are placed in three areas around the rim and some of the bottoms of the leaves enter the well.

English, marked as above, Mk. 718, Reg. #272768, L.V., c. 1897

DEVON

made by Alfred Meakin

This plate has an unevenly scalloped edge and its rim is detailed with bow knots and floral embossing. The border is printed with three bouquets of roses that alternate with three clumps of small flowers. These are joined at the bottom by garlands of stems and leaves. The lower part of the bouquets enter the well.

English, marked as above, Mk. 2587, L.V., c. 1907

DOG ROSE

made by Ridgways

The scalloped edge of this plate has a 2" deep embossing of leaf forms and berries all around the rim. The rim is also defined by a ¾" border of dark blue. The bowl shown is printed in two shades of blue with over-scaled wild roses and leaves. A paler background of tiny flowers surrounds the central design.

English, marked as above, Mk. 3312, L.V., c. 1905

DOROTHY

made by W. & E. Corn & Co.

This scalloped little bone dish has a very dark printing of scrolls and sprays. Flowers alternate with pendant forms around its rim.

This pattern is borderline and may not be Flow Blue.

English, marked as above, Mk. 1113, L. V., c. 1901

DRESDEN SPRIGS

made by Robert Cochran & Co.

The border of this plate is printed with small reserves which contain treillage. These alternate with bouquets of peonies and with a single smaller flower. The handles on the dish photographed are heavily embossed.

The center shows one large magnolia and a dahlia, and several smaller flowers with sprays and sprigs.

Scottish, marked R. C. & Co., Mk. 965 M.V., c. 1855-60

DUCHESS

made by W. H. Grindley

This plate has a scalloped gilded edge. Five-petaled flowers are placed asymetrically on the rim. There are smaller sprays across a large group. Sprigs from the larger group enter the well and extend to the center of the plate.

English, marked as above, Mk. 1842, Reg. #184834, L.V., c. 1891

DUDLEY

made by Myott, Son & Co.

The plate photographed has an unevenly scalloped edge with very heavy embossing of shell and wave-like forms. The rim is printed with a dark blue band for ¾".

The entire plate is covered with a picture of two large full blown roses with leaves and buds. Gilt lustre is placed over the embossing on the rim and there is some gold on the center flowers.

English, marked M.S. & Co., Stoke, Mk. 2809, L.V., c. 1898

DUNDEE

made by Ridgways

The scalloped gilded edge of this plate is outlined with small curlicue embossing. The border is printed in Ridgway's typical soft blue. The top of the rim is printed with a pale dahlia-like flower. The bottom of the rim is printed with darker blue flowers and very dark leaves. Sprigs from these enter the well.

English, marked as above, Mk. 3313, L.V., c. 1910

DUNKELD

made by Brownfields Guild Pottery

The edge of this plate is unevenly scalloped, and the design appears only on the border. The pattern is one of trailing flowers and leaves; in two places these are set upon scrolls.

Dunkeld is a small parish in County Perth, Scotland.

English, marked as above, Mk. 669, L.V., c. 1891

EASTERN PLANTS

made by Wood & Baggaley

This plate has an unevenly scalloped edge with a single heavy ridge of embossing. The rim is outlined with three lines of leaves printed at six scallop points. The border design is composed of six different bell-like flowers.

The center pattern is of a stalk with one large bell flower with leaves and buds.

English, marked W. & B., Mk. 4239, M.V., c. 1870

EASTWOOD

made by New Wharf Pottery

The plate photographed has a scalloped edge that is also beaded. A blue border is printed within the edge and there is scroll embossing over this and also a gold line. The pattern is printed in grey blue and the rim is decorated with dainty sprays of small flowers that resemble forget-me-nots, and with leaves and sprays that create a wreath effect. Some of the sprigs enter the well which is defined by a circle of bead embossing.

English, marked as above, Mk. 2886, L.V., 1891

EBOR

made by Ridgways

The scalloped edge of this plate is outlined with a dark blue band. Tiny scrolls are embossed around the outer rim. The border is printed with large pairs of dahlias and these are connected by garlands of tiny flowers.

English, marked as above, Mk. 3313, L.V., c. 1910

EDGAR

made by New Wharf Pottery

The gently scalloped edge of this plate is embossed with chain and fleur-de-lis. The border is printed with a greyish-blue design of small flowers and leaves, the tips of which enter the well.

English, marked as above, Mk. 2886, L.V., c. 1891

EL BRAU

made by Booths

The sauce tureen shown is printed in a slate blue. It has a scalloped edge and is embossed with little ridges. The design is a stylized flower with naturalistic leaves and sprigs. The handles are detailed with heavy scrolls.

English, marked as above, Mk. 451, L.V., c. 1891

FAIRY VILLAS I

made by W. Adams & Sons

This scalloped plate has a border printed with flowers. The background is of point d'esprit set in cartouche forms. Sprigs of the flowers enter the well.

There is no center picture on this pattern. See Fairy Villas II and III.

English, marked as above, like Mk. 31 c.

FLORENTINE

made by S.W. Dean, Ltd.

The plate photographed has an unevenly scalloped edge that is also decorated with beaded embossing. The design appears on the rim only and consists of foliated cartouches decorated with floral swags, these alternate with bouquets that are basically diagonal in shape. Some sprigs and buds enter the well.

English, marked as above, Mk. 1219, Reg. #330453, L.V., c. 1910

FLORIDA

made by Ford & Sons

The little gravy tray photographed has an unevenly scalloped edge that is outlined with printed beading. Over these there has been placed some gold. The border is printed with bouquets of roses and forget-me-nots that alternate with each other. These are set within a lacy net background.

English, marked as above, Mk. 1585, L.V., c. 1891

FLORIDA

made by W.H. Grindley

The edge of this plate is evenly scalloped and is embossed with beading, which outlines the scallops, and it has an inner lining of lace embossing. The rim is decorated with seven bouquets of small rose-like flowers that are linked with garlands of tiny flowers. These garlands drop into the well of the plate.

The center medallion repeats the bouquet motif.

English, marked as above, Mk. 1842, L.V., c. 1891

FOLEY

made by Barker & Kent, Ltd.

The wash basion shown is deeply scalloped and fluted and has a gold edge and scroll embossing. Large peonies and carnations are placed at random around the rim and in the well. Lustre has been sprayed around the rim and over parts of the design.

English, marked as above, Mk. 266, L.V., c. 1891

GARLAND

made by Wood & Son

This plate has a scalloped edge and the scallops are outlined by a gilt circle around the edge. It is further decorated with bead, chain, and fleur-de-lis embossed concentric circles. These are placed on a dark blue ½" band. The rim is embellished with a narrow wreath of acorns and oak leaves, and the well is defined by a garland of the same leaves and acorns.

English, marked as above, Mk. 4285, L.V., c. 1891

GIRONDE

made by W.H. Grindley

This fourteen sided plate is indented slightly. Fleur-de-lis and scroll embossing are placed around the edge, and gold is painted over the details of the embossing. Sprays of peony-like flowers are placed at random around the border and a small flower rests at the side of the well. Gironde is a department in S.W. France and Bordeaux is its capitol.

English, marked as above, Mk. 1842, L.V., c. 1891

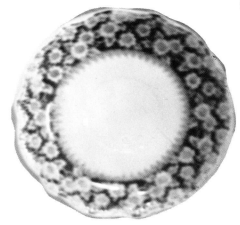

GRACE

made by W.H. Grindley

This plate is unevenly scalloped with an edge that has seed embossing and scrolls that detail the scallops. The border design consists of the entire surface of the rim covered in a dark blue background and sprinkled heavily with small zinnia-like flowers. The well is detailed by fleur-de-lis picketing.

English, marked as above, Mk. 1842, Reg. #303495, L.V., c. 1897

GRENADA

made by Henry Alcock & Co.

This plate is deeply scalloped and has a gilt edge. The border has a blue band that is ¾" wide and is overprinted with flowers. The border is divided in five places by a scroll and flower pattern that form a small stylized pattern. These alternate with sprigs of five different varieties of flowers which are placed around the rim. The stems and leaves from these enter the well. The border outline is detailed in gold.

English, marked as above, Mk. 65, L.V., c. 1891

GROOP "THE"

made by Ford & Challinor

The rim of this plate is outlined by a double blue line of semi-circle hatching. The entire plate is covered with a design of five-petaled flowers that are almost stylized, and small baroque scrolls and sprigs.

The center floral pattern includes a scroll design that resembes a stringed instrument, like a harp.

English, marked F. & C., Mk. 1595A, M.V., c. 1870

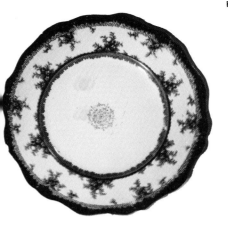

HAMILTON

made by John Maddock & Sons

This plate is unevenly scalloped and is gilt edged. The upper rim is covered with a very dark band that is contained by a Greek key design. The rest of the rim is printed with small bouquets and sprigs. The well is defined by a gold circle on the lower edge of the rim and by a wreath of small lambrequins around the well. In the center there is a gold snow flake type design.

English marked as above, Mk. 2464, L.V., c. 1896

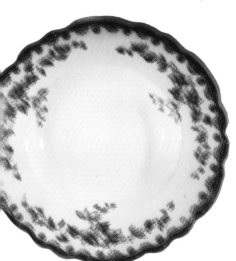

HASTINGS

made by Wedgwood & Co. Ltd.

This plate has an unevenly scalloped edge. Gold lustre has been placed around its rim. Floral and scroll embossing is placed within the rim below the line of lustre. The border is printed with sprays of jasmine and leaves. Some of the leaves enter the well.

English, marked as above, Mk. 4061, L.V., c. 1908

HUDSON

made by J. & G. Meakin

The upper border of this platter has a gilt edge and a row of criss-cross embossing. Right below this there is a dark printed border of large fleur-de-lis over laid with embossed dotted garlands. The rim is printed with large tulips, carnations and dahlias that are linked with smaller flowers and leaves to form a wreath.

The center design is composed of one carnation with buds and a sprig.

English, marked as above, Mk. 2599, L.V., c. 1890

HURON

made by F. Winkle & Co.

The mug shown has an edge outlined with a very dark narrow band. The pattern on the body is of daffodils, ribbon bows, and roses. The mug is embellished with vertical scroll embossing.

English, marked Colonial Pottery, Mk. 4215, L.V., c. 1891

IDEAL

made by W.H. Grindley

This plate is printed in slate blue. It has a gently scalloped edge and some scroll and floral embossing. The border is printed with sprays of wild roses, leaves, and scrolls. Part of this design enters the well.

English, marked as above, Mk. 1842, Reg. #213154, L.V., c. 1893

IOWA

made by Authur Wilkinson

This plate has a scalloped, gilded and beaded edge. There is scroll and floral embossing on the upper part of the rim which is printed in plain deep cobalt. The well is defined by small scallop embossing that has been gilded. The center design is of one full blown rose, a rosebud and leaves and sprays.

This identical design appears as "Blue Rose" by Grindley, and as one of the "Trent" plates by Ford & Son.

English, marked Royal Staffordshire Pottery, Mk. 4170, L.V., c. 1907

IRIS,

made by Clementson Bros.

The boat shaped dish pictured has swirled ridging from its outer gilded edge to the well. The entire plate is blue with the darkest part at the rim shading to light at the center. Printed over this are large iris and leaves. The entire dish was sprayed with lustre.

English, marked as above, Mk. 908, L. V., c. 1905

JANETTE

made by W.H. Grindley

These plates are fourteen sides, the sides are gently curved with embossed rims with scrolls and small pendant designs. The border is outlined with a ½" blue line that is filled with tiny flowers. Groups of four-petaled flowers resembling dogwood are placed around the rim. These extend into the well.

English, marked as above, Mk. 1842, Reg. #292398, L.V., c. 1897

JAQUEMINOT

made by Ridgways

The gently scalloped edge of this plate is outlined by scroll and fleur-de-lis embossing and a printed border. The design is of an over scaled stem of full bloom roses which encircles the entire plate. Jaqueminot is probably the name of a rose.

*English, marked as **above, Mk.** 3310, L.V., c. 1891*

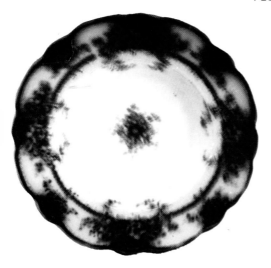

KELVIN

made by Alfred Meakin

This plate has a scalloped, embossed and gilded rim. Floral bouquets of wild roses and sprigs are placed around the rim. The well is outlined by a blue lace-like band for about ½". Some sprigs enter the center. The well is also defined by scalloped and floral embossing.

The center depicts a small bouquet of wild roses, with sprigs and flowers surrounding it.

English, marked as above, Mk. 2585, L.V., c. 1891

KESWICK

made by Wood & Sons

This plate is printed in a greyish blue and has a scalloped edge. It is embossed with scrolls and shell-like forms. The border is printed with baroque cartouche forms that enclose small wild roses. These are connected with a lace-like lattice. Sprigs from the bouquet forms enter the well.

The center depicts a stylized bouquet of four little flat rose forms.

English, marked as above, Mk. 4285, L.V., c. 1891

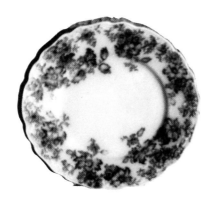

KILLARNEY

made by New Wharf Pottery

This plate has a scalloped edge with scroll embossing. The border is patterned with wild roses, leaves and buds. The buds are placed so as to be completely within the well.

English, marked as above, Mk. 2886, L.V., c. 1891

LA BELLE

made by Wheeling Pottery

This dish has a rippled scallop border that is embossed with vertical ridges and floral designs. A very dark blue band is around the edge and this is decorated with bright gold. Floral sprays are placed around the edge and project into the center. The field of this dish is bluish-white.

American, maked "La Belle China", (Thorn, P. 154), Mk. 28, L.V., c. 1900

LADAS

made by Ridgways

The gently scalloped edge of this plate is gilded. The outer rim is printed with tiny sprigs of buds and leaves. Ten small bouquets of maple-like leaves and petaled flowers are placed so that half of the bouquets enter the well and form a wreath.

English, marked as above, Mk. 3312, L.V.,.c. 1905

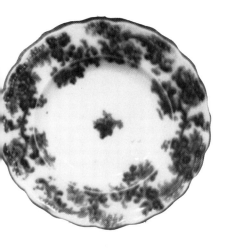

LANCASTER

made by New Wharf Pottery

The scalloped edge of this plate is embossed. A baroque design of scrolls and flowers curves around the rim and enters the well at several places. In the center of the well is a single little flower with a large leaf and tiny sprigs.

English, marked as above, Mk. 2886, L.V., c. 1891

LE PAVOT

made by W.H. Grindley

    This plate has an unevenly scalloped edge and is embossed with a single line around the edge, with further embossing of scrolls and arch-like designs. The border is printed with sprays of poppies and leaves, and the saucer shown has one small poppy printed off-center in the well. "Le Pavot" means "the Poppy".

    English, marked as above, Mk. 1842, Reg. #277089, L.V., c. 1896

LILY

made by Johnson Bros.

    The pitcher shown has a collar with a banding of fine fishnet design. The body of the vessel is embossed vertically with lines that terminate at the top and bottom with leaves. The pattern consists of a large, many petaled lily, drooping on its long stem and slender leaves.

    English, marked as above, Mk. 2177, L.V., c. 1900

LILY

made by Francis Morley & Co.

    This pitcher has seven sides. Its spout is deeply embossed for its whole length. The top of the pitcher and spout are decorated with a narrow border that continues down the handle. The top of the knob is also painted blue.

    The design on the body consists of two large lilies on one stem.

    English, marked F.M. & Co., Mk. 2760, E.V., c. 1850

LILY

made by Ford & Sons

The pitcher shown has a collar of blue that is overlaid with lustre. The pattern is of large day lilies with buds and stems. The pistils of the lilies are enhanced by gold paint. There is heavy scrolled embossing on the body. The collar on the base has a border of the same blue, and lustre, as at the top.

English, marked as above, Mk. 1586, L.V., c. 1900

LINDA

made by John Maddock & Sons Ltd.

This is a scalloped and gilt edged plate. Its rim is printed with groups of forget-me-nots which alternate with a design that is basically spade shaped. There is raised swag embossing that encircles the plate near the outer edge.

English, marked as above, Mk. 2465, L.V., c. 1896

LOBELIA

made by G. Phillips

This plate is paneled and has fourteen sides. Its edge is outlined by a ring of a spear-like pattern. The border is printed with a running heavy vine on which are leaves, berries, and tendrils. The bottom of the border design enters the deep well.

In the center are three large lance-shaped flowers and their leaves. Lobelia is a woody plant that has scarlet, blue or white flowers, and is of trailing habit.

English, marked as above, Mk. 3012, E.V., Dated June 19, 1845

LORCH

made by S. Hancock & Son

NOTE: The name of this pattern is Larch which is a coniferous tree of the group such as pine, fir and spruce. The design consists of sprays of pine needles.

English, marked as above, Mk. 1932, L. V., c. 1906

LORRAINE

made by Ridgways

The bone dish shown has a scalloped and gilt edged rim. The border is printed with a wreath of scrolls and sprays of roses.

English, marked as above, Mk. 3312, L.V., c. 1905

NOTE: Lorraine is borderline and may not be Flow Blue.

LOUISE

made by W.H. Grindley

This plate is unevenly scalloped and comb tooth embossing has been placed on the top part of the rim. The border is decorated with sprays of roses, and the buds and leaves from these enter the well at three points.

English, marked as above, Mk. 1842, L. V., c. 1891

LUCERNE

made by J. Dimmock & Co.

The rim is gently scalloped and gilded around the edge. There are delicate tracings of stems and groups of three small flowers.

The backstamp is marked "Cliff", because after 1878 the proprietor of Dimmock Co. was W.D. Cliff and his name appears on most of that company's marks.

English, marked Cliff, Mk. 1293, Reg. #221056, L.V., c, 1893

LUGANO

made by Ridgways

This plate is printed in Ridgways' soft blue. The rim is scalloped and is outlined with a 1/2" ridge of embossing and gilding. This embossing forms a gadroon edge. The border is paneled and printed in five areas with small bouquets of little flowers and leaves. Tendrils from one bouquet invade and cross the center of the well. There is some gilding on the flowers and leaves.

English, marked as above. Mk. 3313, L.V., c. 1910

LUZERENE

made by Mercer Pottery

The rim of this plate is outlined by a dark narrow band that has fleur-de-lis printed in it. The saucer shown has a border of dahlias and very dark leaves set within printed scallops.

The center pattern is a circular bouquet of dahlias and leaves placed over a central blue circle composed of heart shaped forms.

American, marked as above, Mk. (See Thorn, P. 138, Mk. 24. 27, & 29, any of these marks appears ɔn Luzerene), L.V., c. 1890

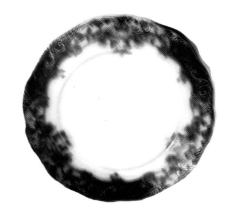

MANHATTAN

made by Henry Alcock

This is a twelve sided plate and the sides are slightly indented. The edge is encircled by scroll and wave like embossing. The border is printed with alternate dark and light panels of cobalt, which contain daisy-like flowers and leaves. Those in the lighter panels extend into the well. A narrow band of dots is placed midway on the rim.

English, marked as above, Mk. 65, L.V., c. 1900

MARECHAL NIEL

made by W.H. Grindley

This plate is unevenly scalloped, has feather embossing, and a dark blue band encircles the rim. The pattern consists of sprays of roses, rose buds, stems and leaves, all placed in asymetrical positions around the platter shown. One stem of roses is placed off-center in the well.

Marechal Niel is the name of a large, medium yellow rose that produces in clusters. It is in the Noisette class of roses, popular at the turn of the century in the southern United States and Europe. These roses do not live in cold climates. Very few samples of the rose remain today, but the Marechal Niel was considered one of the finest roses in the world.

English, marked as above, Mk. 1842, Reg. #263030, L.V., c. 1895

MARGUERITE

made by W.H. Grindley

This plate has a scalloped rim that is sometimes gilt edged. Bouquets of daisies, which are called "Marguerites" in England, are placed around the border in six places and are connected with tiny sprigs and rounded buds. Sprays from the bouquets enter the well.

English, marked as above, Mk. 1842, L.V., c. 1891

MARTHA

made by Bridgett & Bates

The scalloped rim of this plate is enhanced with comb tooth embossing and with little uniting scrolls around the edge. The design is principally of basket-like forms filled with small bouquets of five-petaled flowers. These are placed around the border and are connected by sprays and scrolls.

The center design is a basket and a bouquet.

English, marked as above, Mk. 587, Reg. #288120, L.V., c. 1896

MEISSEN

made by Libertas

The pattern on the plate is composed of scrolls in triangular arrangement that alternate with fleur-de-lis on the border. Small bouquets are placed under the fleur-de-lis, and in the center a bouquet is supported by a basket shaped trelliage. This is exactly the same pattern as "Meissen" by Mehlen.

Prussian, marked as above with an eagle mark, L.V., c. 1891

MEISSEN

made by F. Mehlem

The bowl photographed has heavy embossed scrolled lines that divide it into five sections. The rim of the bowl is embossed in a circular star-like design. The border is printed with floral bouquets set in blue scrolls that are placed over the embossing and form closed reserves.

The center design is a bouquet similar to those in the reserves, and is composed of wild roses and leaves, and forget-me-not sprays, set upon a small scrolled trellis.

German, marked F.M. Bonn, L.V., c. 1891

MELBOURNE

made by W.H. Grindley

This plate has a gently and evenly scalloped rim with a dark blue edge that is outlined with beading and is embossed for 1/4" with scrolls. On the rim are small panels of trellis that alternate with slightly larger panels containing a carnation and bud design. On some plates gilt has been applied around the design and the edge.

English, marked as above, Mk. 1842, L.V., c. 1900

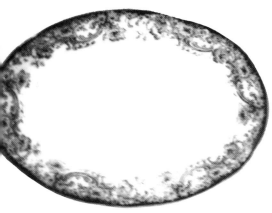

MELROSE

made by Doulton

This plate has a gently scalloped edge that is gold rimmed. The patterns appears on the rim only and consists of baroque scrolls, large six-petaled flowers, and smaller shaggy chrysanthemums.

English, marked as above, Mk. 1332, Reg. #316429, L.V., c. 1891

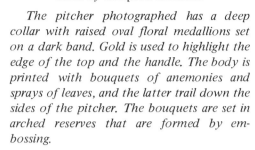

MELTON

made by Sampson Hancock

The pitcher photographed has a deep collar with raised oval floral medallions set on a dark band. Gold is used to highlight the edge of the top and the handle. The body is printed with bouquets of anemonies and sprays of leaves, and the latter trail down the sides of the pitcher. The bouquets are set in arched reserves that are formed by embossing.

English, marked as above and "Opaque China", Mk. 1933, L.V., c. 1910

MENTONE

made by Alfred Meakin

This plate is printed in greyish blue and has a very gently scalloped edge. Its rim is detailed by a narrow circle of tiny flowers. The border is printed with bouquets of poppies and daisies, and these are joined by scrolls that enclose fine net.

English, marked as above, Mk. 2585, L.V., c. 1891

MERION

made by W.H. Grindley

This plate is printed in greyish blue ink, and is scalloped and embossed. Its rim is outlined in a 1/2" border of a straight blue line. Baroque curves divide the dish shown into four sections. The division designs are stylized spade shapes, and a fairly large realistic rose and bud are placed in each space. There is some gold on the scrolls and flowers.

English, marked as above, Mk. 1842, Reg. #292307, L.V., c. 1897

MESSINA

made by Cauldon Ltd.

The rim of this plate is divided by eight large blue rimmed scallops and its edge is lightly embossed. Three heavy leaf patterns are placed around the rim and these alternate with three floral patterns of asters and chrysanthemums. Some sprigs from the bouquets enter the well.

The center of the plate shows a small single stemmed spray of three small flowers.

English, marked as above, (See Kovel, Pg. 248, Mk. M), L.V., c. 1905

MESSINA

made by Alfred Meakin

This plate is gently scalloped and its edge is outlined with gilt. There is some ridge and scroll embossing around its edge. Sprays of flowers resembling asters are placed around the rim, most predominantly on one side, and these extend into the well.

English, marked as above, Mk. 2586, L.V., c. 1891

MIKADO

made by W. & E. Corn

The unevenly scalloped edge of this plate is gilded. There is some scroll embossing around the rim. Its outer border is printed with a diaper pattern of trellis and flowers. Three large reserves are joined by scrolls that contain bouquets of small nasturiums and sprays.

The center picture is a bouquet design composed of the flowers, sprigs, and scrolls.

English, marked as above, with "Porcelain Royal," Mk. 1113, L.V., c. 1900

MILLAIS

made by Sampson Hancock

This relish dish is slightly indented, and this forms scallops. Its edge is printed with small five-petaled flowers. Sprays of roses in full bloom, with leaves and buds, are placed on either side of the dish. There is some embossing of sprays and fleur-de-lis.

Millais was an English painter who was elected president of the Royal Academy in 1896.

English, marked as above, Mk. 1932, L.V., c. 1906

NOTE: This pattern is borderline and may not be Flow Blue.

MONTANA

made by Johnson Bros.

This bone dish is printed in greyish blue and has a scalloped edge. Its rim is outlined with a fine net design and small flowers and scrolls. Peonies alternate with daffodils around the border. The well is outlined with a picket design and blue flowered band.

English, marked as above, Mk. 2177, L.V., c. 1900

MORNING GLORY

made by Thos. Hughes & Sons

This plate is gently and unevenly scalloped, and has a gilded edge. Its border is detailed at top with curvilinear comb-like embossing. The rim is printed in three places with groups of morning glories and a baroque scroll. A few floral buds enter the well.

English, marked as above, Mk. 2122, L.V., c. 1895

MORNING GLORY

made by John Ridgway & Co.

The plate shown has an unevenly scalloped edge with a dark printed band of running curves. Five morning glories with their stems and leaves form a wreath around the border.

The backstamp is impressed "Stoneware" and the mark is the Royal Coat of Arms.

English, marked as indicated, Mk. 3258, E.V., c. 1845

MOSS ROSE (I)

maker unknown

This plate has fourteen panels and its outer edge is not scalloped, but the edge around the well is scalloped in reverse. These reverse scallops form lines that run outwards from the well to the edge and form panels. The edge is printed with running curves that are threaded with a line that is painted red. The border is printed with groups of two or three roses. These are colored with green, henna red, and yellow.

The center shows a large rose with buds and leaves, and a stem of bell flowers. These are all over-painted with the above named colors.

The backstamp states merely "Moss Rose" and is outlined in a wreath of the same flowers.

English, E.V., c. 1850 – 1860

MOSS ROSE (II)

maker unknown

This plate has a scalloped edge, its outer rim is bordered with a design of small circles and scallops. The rim is printed with three sprigs and three Moss Rose buds.

The center design shows one long stemmed rose in full bloom with a bud. The bud is covered by the furry sheath that gives this rose the name.

English, no mark, M.V., c. 1870 – 1880

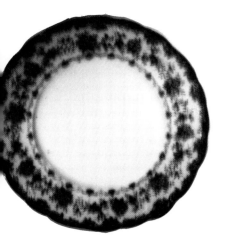

McKINLEY

made by Samuel Ford

The scalloped edge of this plate is enhanced with a very dark blue narrow banding around the edge. There is scroll embossing at five points around the rim. A design of iris blossoms, large leaves, and buds and branches cover the entire border. It is contained at the top rim by a scroll pattern, and at the bottom and around the well by a wreath of scrolls and leaves.

English, marked as above, Mk. 1604, L.V., c. 1900

NANKIN

made by Davenport

This is a stylized oriental design of lotus blossoms. The edge is printed in terra cotta red, and the same red is used in over-painting on the flowers and buds.

Nankin was the ancient capitol of China.

English, impressed anchor mark, printed mark as above, Mk. 1184, E.V., c. 1850

NANKING

made by Doulton

This is a pattern that contains henna red flowers, as does Nankin.

English, marked as above, Mk. 1329, L.V., c. 1900

NEOPOLITAN

made by Johnson Bros.

This plate has an unevenly scalloped edge, which is decorated with scroll and shell embossing. The pattern is placed over the border and well asymetrically, and is composed of scrolls and sprigs and peony-like flowers.

English, marked as above, Mk.· 2177, L.V., c. 1900

NORWICH

made by W.H. Grindley

The backstamp is very blurred on this bone dish, and only a few letters of the name are legible, so this may not be the correct name.

The dish has a scalloped, beaded edge with floral embossing. The design consists of wreaths of Canterbury bell-like flowers and tiny roses. The well is enhanced by a circle of tiny embossed, scrolled scallops.

English, marked as above, Mk. 1842, L.V., c. 1891

NOTE: The name Norwich is incorrect. This pattern is Ashburton.

OLYMPIA

made by W.H. Grindley

The scalloped edge of this plate is gilded and has an embossing of scrolls and feathers. Sprays of tiny roses are placed around the border and some sprigs from these enter the well.

This pattern is exactly the same as "Catherine", and as "Catherine Mermot", and has the same registration number.

English, marked as above, Mk. 1842, Reg. #233436, L.V., c. 1894

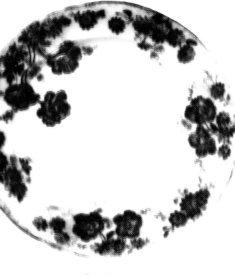

OSBORNE

made by Ford & Sons

This gilt edged, scalloped plate has lustre placed over the upper rim. It is embossed with some scroll and flower designs near the edge. The border is covered with a design of poppies and daisies, and some of this pattern enters the well.

English, marked as above, Mk. 1585, L.V., c. 1893

OSBORNE

made by W.H. Grindley

The rim of this plate is deeply scalloped, and it has embossed beading on the edge, and an inner circle of embossed tiny flowers. The border design consists of cartouche forms that alternate with bouquets of small chrysanthemums. The edge of the well is defined by a row of lacy embossed scallops and sprigs from the bouquets enter the well.

English, marked as above, Mk. 1842, L.V., c. 1900

OSBORNE

made by Ridgways

This plate is slightly scalloped and has a pattern on its border only. This design is composed of floral pendants of chrysanthemums and buds, which alternate with "V" shaped cartouche forms composed of chrysantheumums, leaf sprays, and buds. The latter enter the well and form a circular enclosure around the well.

English, marked as above, Mk. 3312, L.V., c. 1905

OVANDO

made by Alfred Meakin

The scalloped, embossed edge of this plate is enhanced by a banding 1/2" thick of dark blue, which is placed over embossing. The rim is decorated with three large full blown tea-roses, that alternate with two wild roses. These elements are linked with a chain of little scrolled lines.

English, marked as above, Mk. 2586, L.V., c. 1891

 ## PANSY

made by Samuel Ford & Co.

The platter shown is gently scalloped and its outer edge is detailed with a row of small circles. The border is printed with triangular medallions that contains a bouquet in which large pansies are prominently centered. These alternate with inverted tirangular reserves that contain hanging baskets of flowers, and with shield shape designs filled with diaper pattern of little dotted squares. These diverse elements are linked with garlands of beading.

English, marked S. F. & Co., Mk. 1604, L.V., c 1910

NOTE: The name Pansy is incorrect. This pattern is Lonsdale.

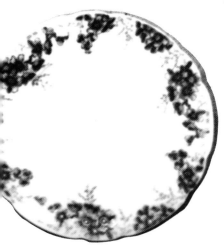

PEACH

made by Johnson Bros.

This plate has a scalloped edge and its border is printed with peach blossoms. The blossoms are outlined with gold. Some sprigs from these enter the well at three places.

English, marked as above, and Royal Semi-Porcelain, Mk. 2177, L. V., c. 1891

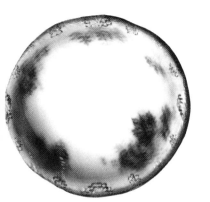

PEONY

made by Alfred Meakin

This bowl has an embossed and gently scalloped, gilded rim. Large realistic groups of peonies are placed around the rim. A pitcher observed was rococo in design. Only the bowl of the pitcher and bowl set is shown.

English, marked as above, Mk. 2589, L.V., c. 1891

POPPY

made by W.H. Grindley

The plate photographed has an unevenly scalloped edge and is printed asymmetrically with large poppies at one side and a few buds and flowers on he other. Some gold is used to highlight the pattern.

English, marked as above, Mk. 1842, L.V., c. 1891

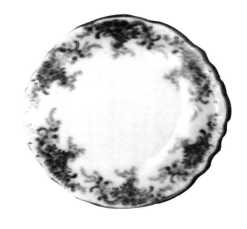

PROGRESS

made by W.H. Grindley

The gently scalloped rim of this plate is edged in gold, and embossed with straight lines toward the center, interspersed with reverse "S" curves. There are six basket-like patterns placed around the rim; all these form triangular based bouquets of small flowers, with sprigs pointing toward the center of the plate, and tendrils that extend into the well.

English, marked as above, Mk. 1842, Reg. #233435, L.V., c. 1894

QUEEN'S BORDER

made by William Adams & Co.

The plate has an unevenly scalloped edge with scroll and shell embossing placed around the upper rim. The border is printed with bouquets of daisies and roses. These are connected with long foliated scrolls. Some sprigs enter the well. Gold is used to center the flowers and on the scrolls.

English, marked as above, Mk. 28, L.V., c. 1891

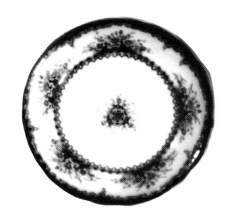

REGALIA

made by Thos. Hughes

This plate has an unevenly scalloped edge and its outer rim is covered with very dark blue for 1/2"; this is held in place by dotted scrolls. The border is printed with five bouquets of jonquils. The well is defined by a double lace-like edging.

The center design is of a circle containing a six pointed star, which is on a dark shield shaped background that is surrounded by sprigs.

English, marked as above, Mk. 2212, L.V., c. 1895

RICHMOND

made by Alfred Meakin

The rim of this saucer is slightly scalloped, its edge is embossed with a shell-like pattern and with scrolls. The border design consists of baroque patterns in dark blue that alternate with floral groups in lighter shades. Sprigs from the floral groups enter the bottom of the plate.

English, marked as above, Mk. 2586, L.V., c. 1891

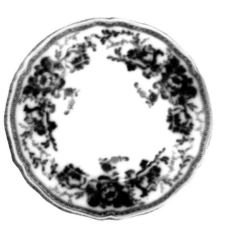

RICHMOND

made by Johnson Bros.

This plate has a gently scalloped edge that is outlined with ridged embossing. The embossing is over printed with a 1/4" border of little dots. The rim of the plate is covered with three groups of large dahlia-like flowers and leaves. These are connected with sprigs. The budgs, flowers, and stems enter the well at three points.

English, marked as above, Mk. 2177, L.V., c. 1900

RIPON

made by F. Winkle & Co.

The biscuit jar shown has a design of overscaled poppies and branch stems, which cover each side of the body.

English, marked F.W. & Co., Mk. 4213, L.V., c. 1900

RIPON

made by Wood & Hulme

This scalloped, shallow bowl has deep embossed fluting around the rim. It is also deeply embossed with curling ribbons and pointed shapes. The fluting is dark blue overlaid with gold lustre. Groups of dahlia-like flowers are placed asymetrically on the dish.

English, marked W. & H., Mk. 4273, L.V., c. 1885

ROMA

made by Wedgwood & Co. Ltd.

This plate has a scalloped edge with tiny scrolls. It is printed in a dark greyish-blue. The border is printed with four groups of peonies and leaves alternating with very dark triangular reserves, which contain roses. Gold is used to highlight the reserves.

English, marked as above, like Mk. 4059, L.V., c. 1905

ROMEO

made by Wedgwood Co.

This plate has a gently scalloped edge. Its rim is bordered in a greyish-blue printing for about 3/4", over which are printed small four-petaled flowers, leaves and sprigs. These extend toward the center but do not enter the well.

English, marked as above, Mk. 4061, L.V., c. 1908

ROSALIE

made by J. & G. Meakin

This plate is printed in slate blue, and it has an unevenly scalloped edge with shell and wave-like embossing around the rim. A fine scalloped line details the outer border. Inside the embossing is a scalloped line that has little three-petaled pendant forms hanging from it. Sprays of wild roses are printed on the rim. The well is defined by a Greek-key circle.

In the center is a single wild rose.

English, marked as above, Mk. 2600, L.V., c. 1890

ROSE

made by W.H. Grindley

This is a gently scalloped and gilt edged plate. There is embossing of scrolls and feather-like lines around the edge. The border is printed with sprays and sprigs of wild roses. Some sprigs are placed in the well.

English, marked as above, Mk. 1842, Reg. #213117, L.V., c. 1893

ROXBURY

made by Ridgways

The scalloped embossed edge of this plate is gilded. The border design consists of three large formalized floral designs of poppies that are connected with garlands to bell-like pendants. This plate is embossed with Ridgways' scalloped ridged border, which gives a gadroon effect. The design enters the well. The well is detailed by panel embossing.

English, marked as above, Mk. 3313, L.V., c. 1910

ROYAL

made by F. Winkle

The toothbrush holder shown has a scalloped edge. The pattern is of asters and their stems with buds and leaves. Lustre has been applied around the upper edge and over the top of the flower design.

English, marked "Colonial Potteries", Mk. 4215, L.V., c. 1900

SPLENDID

made by Societe Ceramique

This is exactly the same pattern as "Brunswick" made by Wood & Son.

Dutch, marked as above, with "Maastricht", L.V., c. 1891

SUTTON

made by Ridgways

This plate has the ribbed, embossed, scalloped and gilded edge that gives a gadroon effect. The design is composed of large scaled dogwood-type flowers that are asymetrically placed and almost cover the entire plate.

English, marked as above, Mk. 3313, L.V., c. 1900

SYDNEY

made by New Wharf Pottery

The unevenly scalloped edge of this plate is detailed with scroll embossing. The border is printed with sprays of small flowers that are intertwined with scrolled stems. Some sprigs at the bottom of the flowers enter the well. Gold is used to highlight the stems and flowers.

E nglish, marked as above, Mk. 2886, L.V., c. 1891

TOKIO

made by Keeling & Co.

This plate is printed in a slate blue and has a gently scalloped gilt edge. The border is printed with asymetrical scrolls containing a brocade pattern and stylized poppies. The bottom of the flower designs enter the well.

English, marked K. & Co. B., Mk. 2243, L.V., c. 1886

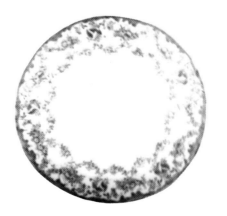

TORBAY

made by Bishop & Stonier

The edge of this plate is slightly gilded and it is printed in a greyish-blue. The border is of intertwining garlands of small roses. Other garlands are swagged to the well fourteen times to form an interior scallop effect. Small conch shells are interspersed with bouquets on the rim.

English, marked as above, Mk. 387, L.V., c. 1900

131

TOURAINE

made by Henry Alcock

This plate has a scalloped gilded edge. The rim is outlined by a 3/4" border of dark and light blue swirls and there is embossing on this. There are five sprays of flowers that are placed around the border, and some of these extend in to the well.

English, marked as above, Mk. 65, Reg. #329815, L.V., c. 1898

TOURAINE

made by Stanley Pottery Co.

Touraine is also found back-stamped Stanley Pottery Co. the pattern is identical but the Stanley version is printed in a darker shade and the blank has a little embossing. Alcock used mark 65 from 1880 to 1910. Colclough & Co. operated the Stanley Pottery from 1887 on and it could be that they first made Touraine for Alcock. The Touraine registry mark dates the design at the end of the year 1898. Possibly Alcock registered the pattern and then later on sold it to Colclough.

English, marked as noted, Mk. 65, Reg. #329815, L.V., c 1898

TRENT (II)

made by Ford & Sons

This plate has a scalloped gilded edge with bead embossing. There is some scroll embossing on the upper rim. The border is printed with very deep cobalt. The well is outlined by a narrow gold circle.

The center design is one large rose with leaves, two buds, and sprigs.

This is exactly the same pattern as "Blue Rose" by Grindley.

English, marked as above, Mk. 4285, L.V., c. 1891

TRILBY

made by Wood & Sons

The scalloped, fluted edge of the dish shown has deep embossing around the border. The rim is also heavily embossed with scrolls, swirls, and shell-like designs. The border is printed with sprays of carnations and budded sprigs.

The center design is of two carnations with sprigs, half contained within a scroll.

English, marked as above, Mk. 4285, L.V., c. 1891

VENICE

made by Johnson Bros.

The scalloped edge of this plate has some feather and scroll embossing. Small dainty sprays of rose-like flowers are arranged around the rim in a pin-wheel effect. The design enters the well and is bordered in the well by a wreath of leaves and scrolls.

English, makred as aboe, Mk. 2177, Reg. #250791, L.V., c. 1895

VERMONT

made by Burgess & Leigh

This plate has a gently scalloped edge. A design of wild roses, leaves and buds encircles the rim, and these enter the well at four points.

English, marked as above, Mk. 717, Reg. #236650, L.V., c. 1895

VERNON

made by Doulton

The jardinere shown has a dark, solid blue collar. Its sides are covered with pictures of large shaggy peony-type flowers, long stems and trailing flowered sprigs.

English, marked as above, Mk. 1332, L.V., c. 1891

VERSAILLES

made by Furnival

This is an evenly scalloped, gilt edged plate. The border is printed with baroque scrolls, which form five semi-cartouche forms in which are depicted five different flowers and leaves. These are connected by a net-like background that is contained by scrolls and by garlands of tiny flowers.

English, marked as above, Mk. 1650, L.V., c. 1894

VICTORIA

made by Wood & Sons

The border on this plate is almost 1" deep in a very dark blackish blue. There is a floral design around the rim which enters the well.

The center design is a circular bouquet with flowers and buds.

English, marked as above, Mk. 4285, L.V., c. 1891

WALDORF

made by New Wharf Pottery

This plate has a scalloped, embossed edge that has shell-like embossing in six places. The border is deeply printed with almost circular flower designs. Some leaves from these enter the well.

The center design is composed of a bouquet of four flowers joined by rose leaves to form a nosegay.

English, marked as above, Mk. 2886, L.V., c. 1892

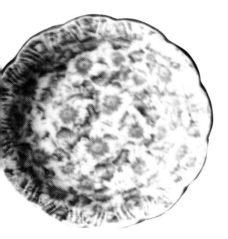

WARWICK

made by Warwick China Co.

This bowl has a scalloped edge with vertical embossing to a depth of 1". There is lustre applied over the embossing. The entire dish is covered with wild roses and leaves.

Observed at an antique show was a plate marked "Warwick China" in a Flow Blue scenic pattern of a water mill with its race.

American, marked as above, (See Thorn, P. 152), Mk. 38, L.V., c. 1900

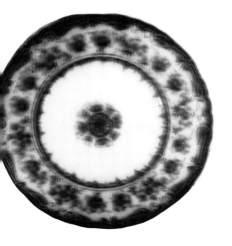

WAVERLY

made by John Maddock & Son

This plate is distinguished by very heavy embossing. Its scalloped edge has a dark blue band for 1/2". The embossing is repeated around the well. The border is printed with poppy-like flowers and sprigs. The well is outlined by a picket design.

The center design is of a small scalloped circle surrounded by flowers and sprigs.

English, marked as above, Mk. 2463, L.V., c. 1891

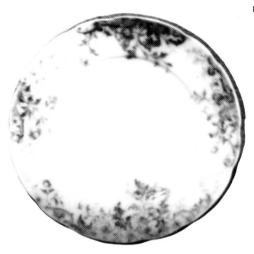

WIND FLOWER

made by Burgess & Leigh

There is a scalloped, gilt edge on this plate and its rim is printed with anemonies, opened and in bud, with their leaves and scrolls. The leaves enter the well at a few points.

English, marked as above, Mk. 718, Reg. #249191, L.V., c. 1895

The following patterns have no pictures available:

ACANTHA

made by J. & G. Meakin

English, L.V., c. 1900

ALDINE

made by W.H. Grindley

English, L.V., c. 1891

ARGYLE

made by Hanley Potteries

This has floral scrolls around the border and some gold trim on the edge of the plate.

English, marked as above, Mk. 1940, L.V., c. 1891

ARGYLE

made by Wood & Son

This pattern is of a floral design on the border only and is decorated with tiny gold bowknots.

English, marked as above, Mk. 4285, L.V., c. 1900

ASTORIA

maker unknown

This is a very deep blue printing and the plates have scalloped rims.

AVA

maker unknown

These plates are of an octagonal shape.

BERWICK

made by New Wharf Pottery

These plates have a gently and unevenly scalloped edge, which is gilt outlined. Scroll embossing encircles the rim. The border is printed with a design of forget-me-nots formed into wreathes, and these alternate with rococo scrolls.

Berwick is a county of Scotland.

English, marked as above, Mk. 2886, L.V., c. 1900

BROOKLYN

made by Maddock & Sons Ltd.

English, L.V., c. 1896

BRUSSELS

made by W.H. Grindley

This design is done in a greyish-blue. The ates have scalloped, beaded, and scrolled 'ges, and the borders are printed with floral uquets alternating with oval garlanded ur-de-lis.

English, marked as above, Mk. 1842, Reg. 03723, L.V., c. 1897

BUTE

made by Ford & Sons

Bute is a name of one of the counties of cotland.

This plate is marked F. & Son Burslem

English, marked as noted, Mk. 1585, V., c. 1900

CAMPION

made by W. H. Gridnley

English, L.V., c. 1891

CAPRI

made by Furnivals Ltd.

The plates have a scalloped edge that is ld lustred, and the design is of large shaggy ter-like flowers.

English, marked as above, Mk. 1651, Reg. 26869, L.V., c. 1891

CATHERINE MERMET

made by W.H. Grindley

This is exactly the same design as "Cath- ine" and "Olympia" by the same maker.

English, marked as above, Mk. 1842, V., c. 1891

CATHLYN

made by Ridgways

This is a dainty design of small flowers ᴜ.. the border only.

English, marked as above., L.V., c 1910

CHARLESTON

made by W.H. Grindley

The plate has a scalloped edge with bead embossing. The border is printed with scrolls that form a baroque design that alternate with bouquets of wild roses. Sprigs from the flowers enter the well. The well is defined by a printed comb tooth design.

English, marked as above, Mk. 1842, L.V., c. 1900

CLARIDGE

made by Alfred Meakin Ltd.

CLIFTON

made by Alfred Meakin Ltd.

This is the same pattern as "Messina" by Meakin.

English, L.V., c. 1891

DEL MONTE

made by Johnson Bros.

The rim of this plate is scalloped and embossed. A dark floral design of jonquils and tiny flower sprigs is placed on the border.

English, marked as above, Mk. 2177, L.V., c. 1900

DORA

made by J. Kent

English, L.V., c. 1900

FLORA

made by H. & J.

The design is composed of silver blue roses. This design covered a bowl observed at an antique show.

Belgium, marked as above, and "Nimy-Belgium", L.V., c. 1891

FLORA

made by Author J. Wilkinson

A plate observed in a show had floral garlands placed around the rim of the plate.

English, marked "Royal Staffordshire Pottery," Mk. 4170, L.V., c. 1907

GLOIRE DE DIJON

made by Doulton

A jardinere observed at a show was printed with a blue beaded scallop border. The entire side of the vessel was covered with a design of very large roses in fill bloom. The pattern name is probably the name of a rose. A similar name, "Gloire de Guilan" is a large damask rose.

English, marked as above, Mk. 1332, Reg. #307815, L.V., c. 1897

HAMPTON

made by Moore & Co.

English, marked "M & Co.", Mk. 2748, L.V., c1890

LANCASTER

made by W. & E. Corn

This is exactly the same pattern as that of New Wharf Pottery but it is made on a different blank; it is unevenly scalloped and the embossing is in long scallops with fan shapes at six points.

English, marked W, L.V., c. 1900

LILAC

made by Dunn Bennett & Co.

The plate has a scalloped gilded edge an the pattern is of the name flower.

English, marked as above, Mk. 142 L.V., c. 1891

MIRA

made by Henry Alcock

English, marked as above, Mk. 65, Re #149950, L.V., c. 1891

NANCY

made by Wedgwood & Co.

A picture observed at a show has ove scaled daffodils on the side panels.

English, marked as above, L.V., c. 190

NAVY

made by Thos. Till & Son

This is a small floral pattern, and th plates are gilt edged.

English, marked as above, Mk. 385 L.V., c. 1891

NIOBE

made by Wedgwood & Co.

Pattern on border only.

English, marked as above, Mk. 405 L.V., c. 1891

NORBERRY

made by Doulton

A vase observed at a show had a plai blue collar. Its sides were covered wit over-scaled poppies on straight vertical stem that were leafed.

English, marked as above, Mk. 135 L.V., c. 1902

PLYMOUTH

made by New Wharf Pottery

The only portion of this plate printed is *e border.*

English, marked as above, L.V., c. 1891

PRINCESS

made by Booths Ltd.

A bowl seen at a show was backstamped as *ove, and was covered in its entirety with* *ver blue flowers.*

English, marked as above, Mk. 451, L.V., *1900*

RUSKIN

made by Cauldon

The border pattern consisted of basket *eave design. The design in the well is* *mposed of flowers and seed pods.*

English, marked as above, L.V., c. 1891

SHELL

made by Wedgwood

This plate is scalloped and has a dark *rinted border of flowers and shells.*

The center pattern is a bouquet.

English, marked as above.

STERLING

made by New Wharf Pottery

This plate has a scalloped edge that is *ilded. The rim is printed with floral car-* *ouche forms. The well is defined by a* *icket border.*

English, marked as above.

TURIN

made by Johnson Bros.

This plate has a floral border that is *1-1/2" wide.*

English, marked as above.

TYNE

made by Bridgwood & Son

English, marked as above, Mk. 594, L.V., *c. 1891*

VIENNA

made by Johnson Bros.

English, marked as above.

VIOLA

probably made by Wood & Baggley

This plate has a gently scalloped edge, *and its border is printed with five long* *horizontal nosegays. These are connected by* *a diaper pattern of small flowers. Some* *sprigs enter the well.*

The center design is a spray of violas with *leaves and sprigs.*

In 1871 a hybrid garden plant, developed *from violets and pansies, was given this* *name. It has a more delicate and uniform* *coloring than pansies.*

English, marked W. & B., could be Mk. *4239, M.V., c. 1875*

WISTERIA

made by Wood & Son

AUTHOR'S COLLECTION

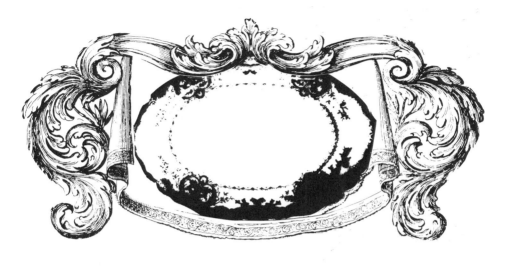

Art Nouveau Category

ALBANY

made by Johnson Bros.

This gently scalloped plate has floral, shell, and bead embossing around the edge. There are six large pointed cartouche forms connected around the border by stylized fleur-de-lis. The details are outlined in gilt. The well is defined by scallop embossing and a small picket design.

The center design is a six sided snowflake pattern. The center dot is gilded.

English, marked as above, Mk. 2177, L.V., c 1900

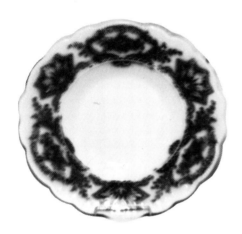

ALASKA

made by W. H. Grindley

This is a deeply scalloped plate and has a beaded and embossed edge. Fan-like forms alternate on the border with baroque cartouches that frame bouquets composed of lemon-like fruit, flowers, and leaves. There is some gold on the design.

English, marked as above, Mk. 1842, L.V., c 1891

ANDORRA

made by Johnson Bros.

These plates are deeply scalloped and have embossed gilded edges. A stylized pair of water lilies and columbine and swirls are deeply printed on the rim in very dark blue and outlined in gilt. These are connected with lightly traced realistic little flower sprigs.

English, marked as above, Mk. 2177, L.V., c 1901

ARGYLE

made by Johnson Bros.

Deeply scalloped edges appear on this plate and they are outlined with scroll embossing. The border is printed in three shades of blue and the rim is divided into three sections, each showing an overscaled water lily, but its leaves are serrated like rose leaves. Three little stylized flowers separate the main designs. Some sprigs and pointed leaves enter the well.

English, marked as above, Mk. 2177, L.V., c 1900

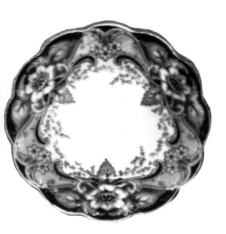

BALMORAL

made by J. &-G. Meakin

This is a multicolored plate. Its rim is scalloped and gilt edged. The border design is composed of turquois colored poppies set within cartouche forms. These alternate with rose colored poppies. A very dark blue border encircles the well which is also detailed with tiny scalloped lines.

The center shows a rose colored poppy set in a Moorish design and enclosed in a circle.

English, marked as above, Mk. 2599, L.V., c 1891

BARONIA

made by Wood & Sons

The bowl shown has an unevenly scalloped edge that is outlined with scroll, scallop and heart embossing on the upper rim. This is 2' deep at four equi-distant points, and is set against a blue printed band. The border is printed with four large reserves formed by an elongated triangular swirling design. In each reserve there is a stylized bell flower, and these are linked at the top with a printed scallop line. A wreath of small vine leaves encircles the well and serves to link the rim design also.

English, marked as above, Mk. 4285, L.V., 1907

BEAUFORT

made by W. H. Grindley

This dish has a scalloped, beaded, and embossed edging around its rim. A pattern of seven inverted hearts surrounded by curved and straight lines are set around the rim. The lines from these extend into the center of the dish. A small snowflake design in the center is encircled by a dark blue ring.

English, marked as above, Mk. 1842, Reg. #408448, c 1903

BERYL

made by Wedgwood & Co. Ltd.

The unevenly scalloped edge of this plate is gilded and an embossed line follows this around the upper rim. The design is on the border only and is a pattern of scrolls alternating with semicircular reserves in which are open double tulips. The lower part of the rim is printed with a stylized design of scrolled ovals connected with scrolled garlands, the bottoms of these enter the well.

English, marked as above, mark 4059, L.V., c 1906

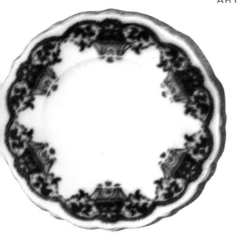

BLUE DANUBE "THE"

made by Johnson Bros.

The edge of this plate is scalloped, embossed with beading, and gilded. The embossing is pronounced. The border carries six stylized designs that resemble arched fire places and over mantles. These are connected with realistic leaves. Some gold has been used to outline the details of these.

English, marked as above, Mk. 2177, c 1900

BRAMPTON

made by Ford & Sons

The pattern on this tureen consists of horizontal rectangles printed with realistic flowers and leaves. These alternate with squares printed with "S" curved designs. These are done on a wide dark blue border that covers the rim. The design appears in a very light blue and in white. There is some gold on this pattern.

English, marked F. & Son, Mk. 1585, L.V., c 1900

BRIAR ROSE

made by Royal Doulton

The jardeniere shown has a collar of plain blue. The bottom band is the same. The design on the body is of stylized large full-blown roses set in arch dividers composed of thorned stems.

English, marked as above, Mk. 1351, Reg. #453404, L.V., c 1905

BROOKLYN

made by Johnson Bros.

These plates are six sided and have a scalloped rim. The edge is outlined by a ½" saw-tooth edge border. Three large stylized daisies alternate with three smaller formalized flowers enclosed in horseshoe cartouche forms. Small sprigs from these enter the well.

English, marked as above, Mk. 2177, L.V., c 1900

BURLEIGH

made by Burgess & Leigh

The vegetable bowl shown has a scalloped gilded edge and there is panel embossing that outlines the design. The pattern is of stylized poppies, the stems of which are caught by swirling bands. The bottom of the design forms a circle around the well.

English, marked as above, Mk. 717, Reg. #413995, L.V., c 1903

CAMBRIDGE

made by Alfred Meakin

This plate has a scalloped edge and its rim is outlined by scroll and floral embossing. This is overprinted in a very dark blue. The rim is divided into six sections and the design consists of spade-like forms that point toward the center. These, in turn, are outlined by floral garlands set within baroque curves that rise to meet and form arch designs.

The center design is of a large six pointed snowflake.

English, marked as above, Mk. 2586, L.V., c 1891

CELTIC

made by W. H. Grindley

The scalloped edge of this plate has some embossing at seven points on the rim. A gold line follows around the edge and outlines the embossing. There is a small fishscale design printed for about ½" deep around the rim which is printed in arch curves and stylized scrolls and leaves.

The center design shows a stylized Celtic cross set in a design of leaves and centered with an eight pointed star.

English, marked as above, Mk. 1842, Reg. #310588, L.V., c 1897

CLIFTON

made by W. H. Grindley

This plate has a scalloped rim with gold edges. The design is on the rim of the plate only and consists of a spade shape pattern that points into the center and alternates with an oval cartouche form. These are done in three shades of blue.

English, marked as above, Mk. 1842, L.V., c 1891

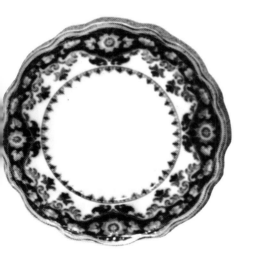

CRUMLIN

made by Myott, Son & Co.

The scalloped, beaded, embossed edge of this plate is also gilded. The border is divided into four triangular cartouches which enclose a stylized flower and leaves. These are connected with dark running bands in which there are flower bud forms. Between each dominant pattern there are set two small stylized lily forms. The well is outlined with a picket design.

English, marked as above, Mk. 2810, L.V., c 1900

DAINTY

made by John Maddock & Son

The unevenly and gently scalloped edge of this plate is embossed with six scrolls and with floral designs. The border is printed with two different cartouche forms; one has a white center and contains small garlands, the alternate is dark centered and contains a spade-like design. The well is marked with fleur-de-lis embossing. Both of the rim patterns enter the well and terminate in a pointed spade-like form.

English, marked as above, Mk. 2464, L.V., c 1896

DELAMERE

made by Henry Alcock

This plate has an unevenly scalloped edge that is gilded. The border design is of a swirling, curved line. The upper rim is covered with small flowers and art designs that fill the scrolls. The lower rim is left open except for the swirls. The bottom of these swirls meet and form a circle around the well.

English, marked as above, Mk. 65, L.V., c 1900

DON

made by Charles Allerton & Son

The unevenly scalloped edge of this plate has a border design that is composed of three large stylized groups of a trio of lilies that hang from a typical art nouveau curvilinear pattern; these alternate with a pair of lilies with long curved stems, which end in scrolls.

English, marked as above, Mk. 88, Reg. #428270, L.V., c 1905

DOUGLAS

made by Ford & Sons

The scalloped edge on this dish is outlined by blue printed loops. The border is printed in a very dark blue background. A stylized pair of flowers are printed in this, and leaves that are almost black, are placed in six different reserves around the border. These are connected with garlanded oval cartouches. Garlands of small flowers are draped between both these patterns and enter the well.

English, marked F. & Sons, Mk. 1586, L.V., c 1891

DUDLEY

made by Ford & Sons

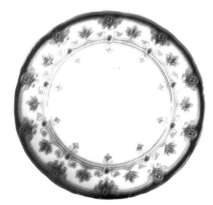

This is a dark slate-blue printing on an unevenly scalloped edge plate. The rim is outlined with a very dark band. The upper border is printed with long curved dotted scrolls that connect small oval medallions, each containing a dark oval design. The lower rim is detailed with stylized lotus blossoms and leaves. These are above a double scalloped inner line. The well is defined by two narrow dark circles and stylized bell flowers that enter the well.

English, marked as above, Mk. 1585, L.V., c 1890

EGERTON

made by Doulton & Co., Ltd.

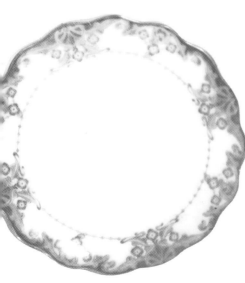

This plate has a scalloped gilt edge. The border design is made up of four heart shaped scrolled cartouches with small four petal flowers around their bases; these alternate with a pattern of scrolls and three of the same little flowers. The pattern is linked by a chain of beading on the lower rim.

English, marked Royal Doulton, Mk. 1351, L.V., c 1905

FLORA

made by Myotts

The pitcher shown has a blue collar around the top of the vase part. A stylized overscaled design of lilies and stems covers the entire body on each side. The collar is lustred and gold is used over the lily design and around the bottom edge and on the handle.

English, marked as above, Mk. 2811, L.V., c 1907

FLORIDA

made by Johnson Bros.

The scalloped, embossed edge of this plate outlines a pattern that is basically six sided. There are three large rounded cartouche forms on the rim which alternate with three angular cartouche forms that are heavily printed in a very dark blue and a lighter shade of blue. A picket border is placed around the well.

English, marked as above, Mk. 2177, L.V., c 1900

FULTON

made by Johnson Bros.

This plate has a scalloped gilded edge. The entire border is printed with stylized trumpet vine flowers in five large clumps. The tendrils from these extend into the well and encircle it.

English, marked as above, Mk. 2177, L.V., c 1900

GENEVA

made by New Wharf Pottery

The gently scalloped rim of this plate is enhanced by a ¼" circle of dotted embossing. The border design of seven tulips is so placed so that their heads dip towards the center.

The center design depicts two tulip blossoms and a bud set in a circular form of tiny rounded bubbles.

English, marked N.W.P., Mk. 2886, L.V., c 1891

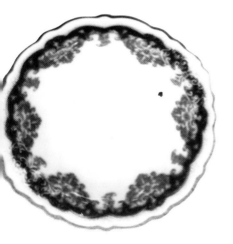

GEORGIA

made by Johnson Bros.

This plate has a scalloped gilted rim with embossed edging that follows the scallops. The border is of a very dark blue on the outer edge and this follows the pattern of scallops. Six large triangles formed of scrolls are placed on the rim and point toward the center, and alternate with small curling single plume-like forms that fall toward the center. The entire design froms a six sided open star shape in the middle.

English, marked as above, Mk. 2177, Reg. #417778, L.V., c 1903

GLADYS

made by New Wharf Pottery

This is a scalloped plate with embossing that follows the scallops in a curved line with six shell-like forms at equal intervals. The border is printed with cartouche forms that enclose embossed shells. Alternating with these are spade-like forms composed of curves and leaves.

English, marked N.W.P., Mk. 2883, L.V., c 1891

HADDON

made by W. J. Grindley

This scalloped edge plate has dotted, floral and scroll embossing around the rim. The border is printed with closed heart shaped medallions that enclose a stylized flower. These alternate with open arch forms that frame the same flower but the design is inverted. The flowers are used between the forms to connect the designs.

English, marked as above, Mk. 1842, L.V., c 1891

HADDON

made by Libertas

This pattern is identical to "Haddon" made by W. H. Grindley.

Prussian, marked as above, L.V., c 1891

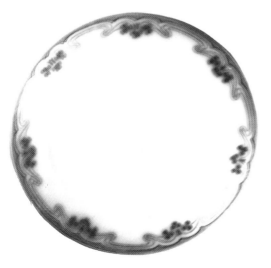

IDRIS

made by W. H. Grindley

The border of this plate is printed with a design of three leaf clovers set in typical Art Nouveau swirls. The outer rim is decorated with a row of little dots. Gold is used to encircle the plate and set off the curved lines of the main design.

English, marked as above, Mk. 1842, L.V., c 1910

IRIS

made by Authur Wilkinson

This plate has a gold edge and a border that has a deep blackish-blue rim design divided into four parts. In these are set stylized iris with gold outlines.

English, marked Royal Staffordshire Potteries, Mk. 4170, L.V., c 1907

KNOX

made by New Wharf Potteries

The plate photographed has a scalloped edge with scroll and lily form embossing. Its border is printed with pendant ovular cartouches that contain a rounded spade-like design and garlands of small flowers. These designs form arches that encircle the well.

The center design is of a six sided snowflake.

English, marked as above, Mk. 2886, L.V., c 1891

LAKEWOOD

made by Wood & Sons

This platter has an unevenly scalloped edge. The border design consists of four large cartouche forms that terminate toward the center in stylized tulips. These are connected by a web of scrolls, leaves and bell flowers. The center well is defined by a lacing of stems that forms a picket design.

English, marked as above, Mk. 4285, Reg. #348700, L.V., c 1900

LEICESTER

made by Burgess & Leigh

The printing on this plate is in a greyish blue. It has a scalloped edge with scroll and floral embossing. The outer rim is printed in a dark blue band that is contained in a ring of dots. The border is printed with flowers and fleur-de-lis forms. The well is defined by a tatting edge on the flange and a comb-like design around the well.

The center design is a six sided snowflake type of pattern.

English, marked as above, Mk. 717, Reg. #364190, L.V., c 1910

LICHFIELD

made by Ridgways

This dish is printed in slate blue. The design on the tureen shown is of wild roses and willow leaves. These are set in oblong panels that are decorated with a fan-like design that is curved on the ends. These panels are separated by smaller enclosed areas that are entirely covered with flower sprays. A stylized border of leaves circles the top of the tureen.

English, marked as above, Mk. 3310, Reg. #114297, L.V., c 1880

LORNE

made by W. H. Grindley

The edge on this plate is scalloped and is enhanced by printed beading. There are embossed scrolls around the outer rim at a ½" depth. Small groups of four three-leaf clovers are placed around the border in six places. These are connected by a narrow ribbon-like line. The center of the well is outlined by a narrow stripe, and shows a stylized grouping of the same clovers.

English, marked as above, Mk. 1842, L.V., c 1900

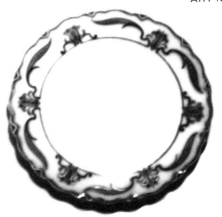

LOTUS

made by W. H. Grindley

This plate is scalloped and gilt edged. Formalized lotus flowers and long slim leaves are printed on the rim. There is some gold along the edges of the leaves. A circle on the flange outlines the well.

English, marked as above, Mk. 1843, L.V., c 1910

LYNDHURST

made by W. H. Grindley

The border of this plate is printed with scalloped lines. The outer edge is filled in with a pattern of a flower and of little straight lines. Within the scallops formed by this outer border are triangular designs composed of scrolls and a flower. These alternate with a pendant design made of scrolls at the top and three small flowers at the bottom. These designs just enter the well.

English, marked as above, Mk. 1842, L.V., c 1891

MADRAS

made by New Wharf Pottery

The plate photographed has a scalloped and embossed beaded edge. Over this has been printed a very dark blue border. The rim is printed with curvilinear designs and scrolls and tiny floral sprays. The well is defined by a circle of picket design.

The center design is a stylized three part pinwheel.

English, marked as above, Mk. 2886, L.V., c 1891

MALVERN

made by F. Winkle

The scalloped edge of this plate is outlined with floral embossing over printed flowers. The border is printed with bouquets of ruffled poppies, and these are separated by a shell-like swirl design. The well is outlined by a circle of stylized ribbons and hearts.

English, Marked Colonial Pottery, Mk. 4215, Reg. #406306, L.V., c 1903

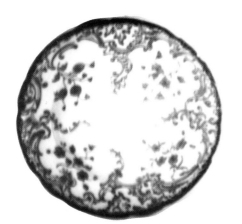

MARIE

made by W. H. Grindley

This plate has a scalloped edge with a ½" deep dark blue border. The design is composed of baroque swirls and scrolls. These form a framing for four groups of naturalistic five petaled flowers, stems, and buds. Both elements of the design enter the well.

English, marked as above, Mk. 1842, Reg. #250387, L.V., c 1891

MILFORD

made by Burgess & Leigh

A grey-blue printing appears on this plate. The top of the tureen shown has a scalloped gilded edge. The design on the top is made of a border strip with small white dots. This is contained by scalloped gold lines. Stylized leaves and fleur-de-lis are placed on all four sides of the top and on the corners of the dish below.

English, marked as above, Mk. 718, Reg. #565728, L.V., c 1910

MURIEL

made by the Upper Hanley Potteries

This plate has an unevenly scalloped and gilded edge. The upper border has a narrow diapered rim. There are five heart shaped designs on the rim which alternate with a single large realistic peony. These are joined by small garlands of sprigs and buds. The lower part of the border design enters the well.

The center design is a stylized peony with leaves.

English, marked as above, Mk. 3928, L.V., c 1895

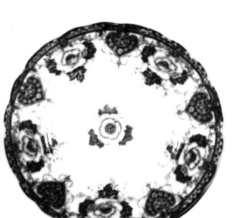

NANCY

made by Grimwades Ltd.

The registry mark shown is later than the backstamp mark, which merely reads "Stoke on Trent". The pattern was registered in 1900 but the plates had to be labeled "England" after 1891. This is an oddity.

The plate shown has an unevenly scalloped edge and is detailed with a dark band contained by scrolls and flowers. The border is printed with three Art Nouveau cartouche forms that are framed with small five petaled flowers. These alternate with horizontal sprays of water lilies with trailing stems. The bottom of both patterns enter the well.

English, marked Stoke on Trent, Mk. 1823, Reg. #359029, L.V., c 1900

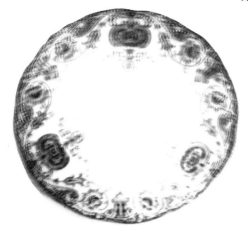

NAVARRE

made by Wedgwood

The plate photographed has a scalloped gilded edge. Fine-line scroll embossing and shell embossing are placed at six points around the rim and there is bead embossing to further enhance these. The border design consists of three cartouche forms, somewhat heart shaped, from which small heart designs are pendant. These alternate with smaller stylized heart and flower motifs. Gilt outlines both the hearts and the flowers.

English, marked as above, Mk. 4059, L.V., c 1905

OREGON

made by Johnson Bros.

The small individual vegetable dish shown has a scalloped, beaded edge. There are double blue scallop lines printed at the top of the border. A formalized poppy design appears on the rim. This design is so made that the three largest poppies are placed in a design of leaves and buds. The bottom of the design enters the well.

English, marked as above, Mk. 2177, L. V., c 1900

OXFORD

made by Ford & Sons

This plate has a scalloped gilded edge. The border is printed with a reverse heart design and small stylized tulips. These designs are joined at the bottom with scrolls and form a circle around the well.

English, marked as above, Mk. 1585, L.V., c 1900

PARIS

made by New Wharf Pottery

also made by
Stanley Pottery Co.

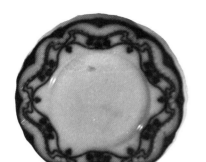

This plate has an unevenly scalloped edge. The border design is detailed by elaborate embossing that forms scallops of white lace-like texture. The printing on the rim forms ribbon-like scrolls in which are placed a trail of three-leaf-clovers. A single small clover alternates within these scrolls.

Paris is also found with the backstamp of the Stanley Pottery. The pattern and the blank are identical. Probably Colcloughs, who owned the Stanley Pottery, obtained the pattern when New Wharf ceased operations in 1894.

English, marked as above, Mk. 2886, L.V., c 1891

PERSIAN

made by Johnson Bros.

The scalloped edge of this plate is outlined with floral, bead and scroll embossing. The rim is enhanced by a little stitching pattern in dark blue. The border is printed with four large cartouches. Between them are sprays of stylized water lilies and other flowers. The well is defined by a picket design.

English, marked as above, Mk. 2177, L.V., c 1902

POPPY

made by New Wharf Pottery

This plate has an unevenly scalloped edge and a circle of ribbon and bows embossing is placed around the rim. The border is printed with large open poppies and swirls of stems, leaves and buds.

English, marked N.W.P., Mk. 2883, L.V., c 1891

POPPY

made by Wedgwood & Co.

The rim of this plate is very dark and is outlined in gilt. There are three large stylized poppies on the plate rim, and these alternate with a pointed bud form. The bottoms of the poppies enter the well.

English, marked as above, Mk. 4060, L.V., c 1908

PORTMAN

made by W. H. Grindley

This deeply scalloped plate has a beaded and gilded edge. Floral embossing encircles its rim. There are cartouche forms of scrolls, each containing a little flower, placed around the rim in three places. Scrolls follow the top of the border and connect the cartouches, and floral sprays are placed around the border also. The well is detailed by lace embossing on the rim, and the design enters the well from all three of the main points of the design.

English, marked as above, Mk. 1842, L.V., c 1891

PORTSMOUTH

made by New Wharf Pottery

The plate photographed has a scalloped, gilded edge. The border is printed with semi-heart shapes that are garlanded. These alternate with triangular forms composed of scrolls. The well is defined by a ½" border of blue and gold.

English, marked as above, Mk. 2886, L.V., c 1891

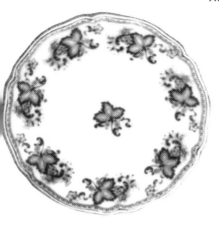

PRINCETON

made by Johnson Bros.

This unevenly scalloped plate appears six sided. Comb-tooth embossing further details the six large scallops. The border is printed with three-leaved ivy forms embellished with leaved scrolls and little flowers. In the circle of the well is a single ivy leaf with two little flowers and three small scrolls.

English, marked as above, Mk. 2177, L.V., c 1900

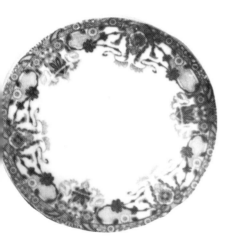

RALEIGH

made by Burgess & Leigh

This plate has a very gently scalloped edge, its rim is outlined by a circle of small flowers and leaves. The border of the plate is printed with three horse shoe shaped forms that frame a stylized daisy. These alternate with three oblong shapes that enclose a lily. These elements are connected by a design of leaves, flowers and an oval of net. The six main designs penetrate the well.

English, marked as above, Mk. 717, Reg. #393237, L.V., c 1906

REGENT

made by Johnson Bros.

The sugar bowl photographed is printed with a very dark blue dotted collar. The design on the body is composed of heart shaped foliated reserves in which there are lily forms, and with scrolled kidney shaped designs from which there is a hanging lily head, and which are surmounted with a fan design.

English, marked as above, Mk. 2178, L.V., c 1910

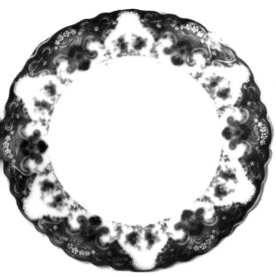

REGENT

made by Alfred Meakin Ltd.

This plate has an unevenly scalloped edge, Floral and bowknot embossing is set on the upper rim, and large swirl embossings descend from the edge to the well at six places around the rim. The border is printed with six scrolled triangular forms. The openings between these are filled with small floral bouquets of sprigs and forget-me-nots. The well is outlined by a row of scrolled floral embossing that is placed on the bottom part of the rim.

English, marked as above, Mk. 2586, L.V., c 1897

REGENT

Maker unknown

This plate has embossing around the edge. The pattern consists of four reserves formed by four vertical stylized flowers and scrolls. In each reserve there is a bouquet.

Probably English, marked "Regent" in a cartouche, L.V., c 1900

REGOUT'S FLOWER

made by Petrus Regout

The bowl shown has a stylized design of fans of leaves that alternate with a group of three stemmed flowers and three leaves. The top border inside the bowl has a small cross hatching design.

Dutch, marked P.R., L.V., c 1900

160

ROSEVILLE

made by John Maddocks

The edge of this plate is scalloped and is bordered with a narrow rim of overlapping semi-circles. The rim of the plate carries a design of stylized peonies flanked by very dark leaves.

The center design is a very stylized flower flanked by naturalistic dark leaves.

English, marked as above, Mk. 2463, L.V., c 1891

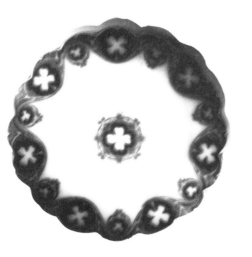

ROYSTON

made by Johnson Bros.

These plates are twelve sided and their edges are outlined with a blue band that is dotted on the inner side. The rim design consists of six different groups of stylized bell flowers. These are joined by looped lines.

English, marked as above, Mk. 2177, L.V., c 1891

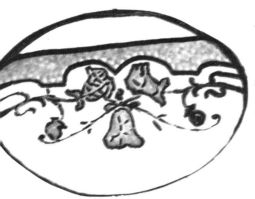

SAVOY

made by Johnson Bros.

This plate has a deeply scalloped edge that is detailed with line embossing. The rim is printed with four-leaf clovers set in oval medallions.

The center drawing is of a four-leaf clover surrounded by a design of scrolled grill work.

English, marked as above, Mk. 2177, L.V., c 1900

SEVILLE

made by New Wharf Pottery

The plate photographed has a scalloped edge and a ¼" ring of tiny flowers around the rim. The pattern on the border of the plate is formed by alternating cartouche forms and oval medallions containing three daisy-like flowers. Sprays of the same flowers connect these designs. The well is circled by a small floral design. The bottom of the design enters the well and is connected with a scrolled lacy picket border and forms a circle around the well.

English, marked as above, Mk. 2886, L.V., c 1891

STERLING

made by Johnson Bros.

The rim of this plate is embossed and scalloped and gilt edged. The design is on the border of the plate only and consists of small beaded strands forming ovals and alternating with heart shaped designs that are gilt outlined.

English, marked as above, Mk. 2179, L.V., c 1910

TRENT

made by New Wharf Pottery

The unevenly scalloped edge of this plate is embellished with shell and scallop embossing. The plate is printed in two shades of blue and a swirling heart design that incorporates three leaves on the upper border and a spade shaped figure in the middle of the reserve. The border design meets in the center and forms a stylized six petaled circle.

English, marked as above, Mk. 2886, L.V., c 1891

TRURO

may have been made by Minton

The design on this plate is on the border only and consists of stylized flowers and leaves alternating with small dark geometrical drawings. This would seem to be Art Nouveau, but the country of origin is not given, so this dates rather early for the Art Nouveau movement. Truro is the name of the county seat of Cornwall, England.

Probably English, could be Minton's garter mark #2695, M.V., c 1860

VENTNOR

Maker unknown

This platter has a scalloped gilded edge and its border is printed with scrolls that enclose vertical lines alternating with reserves that are printed with a deeply scalloped circles. There are stylized large poppy-like flowers placed around the rim, and their leaves and some scrolls enter the well.

Probably English, marked "Ventnor" in a cartouche, L.V., c 1900

VERONA

made by Alfred Meakin Ltd.

This plate has a scalloped embossed rim. Its border is printed with scrolls and a very dark border that is 1½" deep. The scrolls are detailed with gold. There is embossing around the well of inverted scallops, each containing a little flower. The well itself is fluted and scalloped. Garlands on the rim surround the well.

English, marked as above, Mk. 2582, L.V., c 1891

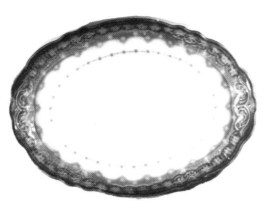

VICTORIA

made by W. H. Grindley

This platter has a scalloped gilded edge. The dark blue edge is set off by beaded embossing. The border is printed with five-petaled flowers and is embossed with pointed arch-like designs. The flower pattern is carried below the embossing and terminates in scallops and fleur-de-lis points. The well is defined by a circle composed of dots and small star-shaped flowers.

English, marked as above, Mk. 1842, L.V., c 1891

WATTEAU

made by Edge Malkin & Co., Ltd.

On the saucer shown the edge is slightly scalloped and is gilded. The rim has a dark blue scrolled band. The border is printed with six cartouche forms that enclose a shell and scale design. These alternate with six open cartouches that are gilded. The well is defined by a series of bell flowers and trefoils that point toward the center. There is embossing around the well.

English, marked as above, Mk. 1445, Reg. #342168, L.V., c 1899

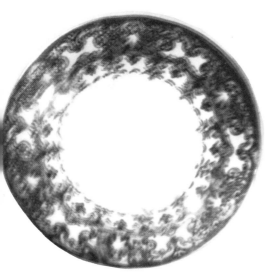

No Picture Available

ATHENS

made by Grimmades Bros.

Reg. #414421, L.V., c 1903

AUBREY

made by Doulton

English, L.V.

CANDIA

made by Cauldon

English, L. V. (This may be an oriental pattern)

CELTIC

Maker unknown

This plate has a scalloped border. On the rim are four repeats of a cross design composed of two ovals interlaced with arching lines.

The center of the plate has a large cross composed of the same design, that of the Celtic Cross.

English, L.V., c 1900

DUCHESS

made by Dunn Bennett

This pattern has an all-over pattern of large dahlia-like flowers. The edge is scalloped and ridged and there was much gilt on the plate observed.

English, marked D. B. & C., Mk. 1421 or 1422, L.V., c 1900

KENSINGTON

made by Keeling & Co., Ltd.

This pattern is composed of three stylized pendant designs that resemble cut prisms. These alternate with three formalized bouquets composed of small stylized flowers set in a three-leaved clover scallop border.

These elements are linked by stylized floral garlands, and loops and flowers descend toward the well from both.

English, marked as above, Mk. 2242, L.V., c 1909

LUCANIA

made by W. & E. Corn

The plate observed had a greyish-blue printing.

English, marked ⟨W⟩, L.V., c 1900

NANCY

maker unknown

A plate observed at a show was printed in grey-blue. The pattern was on the rim only and consisted of five-petaled wild rose type flowers set in stylized ovals with a scrolled border.

English, marked "Nancy", Reg. #399013, L.V., c 1902

OSBORNE

made by T. Rathbone & Co.

The border is printed with groups of three stylized flowers separated by a dragon-fly pattern. The well is defined on the rim by a circle of small geometric designs. There is much oranate gilt trim on this plate.

English, marked T. R. & Co., Mk. 3204, L.V., c 1898

165

AUTHOR'S COLLECTION

Miscellaneous Category

ALMA

made by John Thomson

This plate is fourteen sided and is paneled. The border design is composed of large foliated scrolls that alternate with small bouquets of roses with very dark leaves. The bottoms of both designs enter the well and form a wreath about the center picture. This is dominated by a large urn that is filled with many different flowers. Behind the urn there is a scene of a lake, tall poplar trees at left, and domed buildings and alpine peaks at the right rear.

Scottish, impressed, marked as above, Mk. 3844, E.V., c 1845

ARABIAN

made by Rideway & Morley

This plate has a gently scalloped rim. The pattern is a very dark geometric border on the rim which extends into the well at eight points with mosque "arch-like" forms.

The center design is a star composed of eight arched points. This backstamp mark was used only for six years, from 1836 to 1842.

English, marked R.M.W. & Co., Mk. 3271, E.V., c. 1840

166

AMERILLIA

made by Podmore, Walker & Co.

The plate at hand has a dark outer edge of linked oblong bricks. A band of the same design, but larger, circles the lower half of the rim, and it is possible to see the stylized floral diaper design in these. A floral design wreathes the rim, entwining over and under the oblongs.

The funnel shaped flowers in the center are Amaryllus, hence the name of the pattern.

English, marked P. E. & Co., Mk. 3075, E. V. c. 1850

ARCADIA

made by Enoch Plant

This plate has an edge that is rimmed with a border of small rounded squares, each containing a little six sided star. A tiny triangle of dots points toward the center. There is some gold on the main design which consists of two large rounded cartouche forms enclosing three roses. These have garlands and floral pendants opposite each other and these extend around the center with scrolls and garlands.

English, marked as above, Mk. 3055, L.V., c. 1900

ARGYLE

made by Ford & Sons

The gently scalloped edge of this plate is outlined by a ¼" circle of fleur-de-lis, and its rim is printed with arabesque reserves in which there are lotus and other flowers. These are connected by foliated scrolls. The well is defined by beading and by garlands of floral swags that outline the design and dip into the well.

English, marked as above, Mk. 1585, L.V., c. 1895

ARGYLE

made by W. H. Grindley

This plate is fourteen sided and has small scroll embossing around the edge. The rim is detailed by a single blue line ¼" from the edge. The border is covered with the design of six large curving plumes that are slanted to the left. The tips of these enter the well. The plume design is interspersed with small floral sprays. In some cases gold has been used on this design, but this is not always true.

English, marked as above, Mk. 1842, Reg. #289457, L.V., c 1896

ARGYLL

made by Thos. Dimmock & Co.

Slate blue was used to print this unevenly scalloped plate. Its border is printed with peony-type flowers set in three reserves that reflect an oriental influence, and are formed by scrolls; these alternate with triangular reserves that are bordered with a Greek key design, which also enclose peonies. The bottoms of both elements form a deep circle within the well.

The center picture is of the same flowers with reeds and dark leaves. Argyll is a county of Scotland.

English, marked Pearl Ware, Monogram, Mk. 1300, E.V., c. 1850

ASIATIC PHEASANTS

made by John Meir & Son

The serving bowl photographed has a scalloped edge that is enhanced by a border of printed beading. The upper rim is printed with lined triangular forms that terminate in a flower. The lower border is decorated with six bouquets of peonies and other flowers.

The center design covers the well and is composed of an overscaled bouquet of the border flowers and buds and sprays. On either side of the flowers a bird is perched, each has a crested head and large outstretched wings, and the one at the right has long, curved tail feathers.

English, marked I.M. & Sons, Mk. 2635, M.V. 1865

BEDFORT

made by Ashworth Bros.

The bone dish shown has a rim with a triangular diaper pattern. The border consists of somewhat stylized flowers and leaves. One small insect form is at top right.

English, marked as above, Mk. 140, M.V., c 1870

BELLFLOWER

made by Boch Freres

The bowl shown is decorated with a painted, beaded line at the collar. The body design is of leaves and tiny berries. The pottery that made this dish is an old one that dates from the eighteenth century and was located at Luxembourg, Belguim. The bowl has no name on the backstamp, therefore, this name will be used in order to index.

Belgium, marked as above, (See Kovel p. 206, mark "L" L. V., c 1891

BERKLY

made by Ford & Sons

There is a grey-blue printing on this plate and the rim is outlined with a diaper pattern of small diamonds. The border is printed with eight cartouche forms, each enclosing a rose with buds and leaves. The entire space between the cartouches is covered with a blue dotted background interspersed with small rose blossoms. The bottom of the cartouche ovals enter the well, and these are connected by a row of beading.

English, marked F. & Sons Ltd., Mk. 1586, L.V., c 1908

BERLIN VASE

made by Ridgway

The paneled saucer shown has three medallions set in a border of basket weave. In each medallion is a picture of an urn. Fleurs-de-lis circle the upper and lower edges of the border design.

The center scene shows stone cupids supporting a basin, stone vases full of flowers, and predominantly, a tall handled urn. There are grapes and grape leaves in the foreground. In the left rear can be seen a lake with a boat, and tall trees and buildings are on its banks.

English, marked as above, like Mk. 3269, E.V., c 1850

BLUE BELL

made by Dillwyn-Swansea

This is an eight paneled plate with a pattern of stylized blue bells with long winding stems. The design covers the entire plate.

Welch, marked as above (Imp.), Mk. 3769, c. 1840

BUCCLEUCH

Maker unknown

The wide scalloped edge of this plate is outlined in dark blue. The border is printed with elongated shell motifs that enter half way into the well. The edges of the shell designs are finished with small curling scrolls, and these form and enclose a medallion in which a small flower is pendant.

The center motif is a bouquet of three of the flowers.

Sir Walter Scott, the historic, romantic novelist, was proud of the fact that his ancestors had been border chieftains in Scotland, and that his family head had been the Duke of Buccleuch.

English, dated December 4, 1845, E.V.

CAIRO

made by Barkers & Kent Ltd.

The top of the tureen shown has a scalloped beaded edge. A border of pendant designs are joined at the top by beaded garlands. The well is outlined by a ring of small hearts with leaves and tiny garlands of flowers.

English, marked as above, Mk. 266, L.V., c 1900

CASTRO

made by J. & G. Meakin

This is the same pattern as Colonial by the same maker. The slightly scalloped edge is detailed with blue feather edging, and scroll and wave crest embossing.

The design covers the plate and consists of stylized carnations and stems, so placed as to enter the well at four points. The center design is of a single carnation.

English, marked as above, Mk. 2600, L.V., c 1891

CAVENDISH

made by Keeling & Co.

This is an all-over pattern of floral sprays that give a paisley effect at a distance, but upon close inspection is clearly floral.

English, marked Losalware, Mk. 2245, L.V., c 1910

CHAPLET

made by J. & G. Meakin

This pattern has a scalloped, beaded, gilded edge, which is further enhanced with slight embossing. The border has stylized dainty oak leaves and sprays.

The center design is a wreath of leaves embellished with tiny flowers. The well is outlined by a gold circle that is garlanded. Inside this is another circle of a small scalloped design.

English, marked as above, Mk. 2602, L.V., c 1907

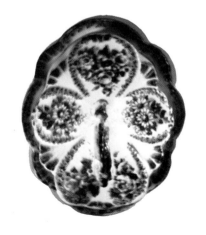

CHEESE DISH

Maker unknown

The oddly shaped top of this dish is scalloped and fluted. It is printed with four bouquets of roses and daisies. The sides of the cover are also printed with the same flowers. Gold is used on the handles and on the fluted scallops. The bottom tray has a narrow floral edge that is gilded.

Probably English, M.V., c 1870

CLOVER

mady by W. H. Grindley

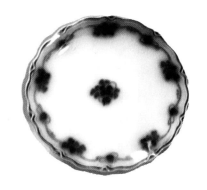

This saucer has a scalloped edge outlined with linear and shell embossing. Three-leaf clovers alternate around the border with blossoms, and these are linked by stylized swirling stems.

The center design consists of four clover leafs with one blossom.

English, marked as above, Mk. 1843, L.V., c 1910

COLONIAL

made by J. & G. Meakin

This plate has a scalloped rim set off by scroll and wave crest embossing. It is identical to the pattern "Castro" described in the preceding text.

English, marked as above, Mk. 2600, L.V., c 1891

CONWAY:

made by New Wharf Pottery

This bowl has a scalloped edge trimmed in blue and some scroll embossing. The pattern on the rim consists of seven stylized onion designs separated by a straight line. These are joined by stylized leaves.

The center design is a snowflake type, a six-sided star with six radiating spokes set within a scalloped circle.

English, marked as above, Mk. 2286, L.V., c 1891

CORINTHIAN FLUTE

made by Cauldon

This slightly scalloped saucer has a border of vertical designs. A floral brocade alternates with a drawing of little berries on branches.

The well is defined by circular lines and by a double fleur-de-lis design. The center pattern is a wheel-like circle made up of the border elements and is outlined with stylized flowers.

English, marked (impressed) Cauldon, Mk. 822, L.V., c 1905

COUNTESS

made by W. H. Grindley

This plate has a scalloped, beaded, and gilded edge. Its rim is printed with blue leaf-like scrolls and small red flowers.

The center design is a small flower outlined by a tracing of curved lines.

English, marked as above, Mk. 1842, L.V., c 1891

CYPRUS

made by Ridway, Bates & Co.

The border design is a quarter inch thick and is in plain blue. The rim is covered with bamboo-like leaves and feathery foliage. Four large detailed butterflies are placed at equal distance around the rim design.

The center scene shows a wading bird on a bank and a smaller bird diving after a dragonfly that skims over the foreground water.

English, marked J.R.B., could by Mk. 3268, M.V., c 1857

DANUBE

made by Charles Allerton & Sons

The oval vegetable dish shown has a gilded and scalloped edge. A narrow border of a scroll and flower design is placed around the rim in two shades of blue. A narrow gold line circles the inside of the bowl. Heavy leaf embossing is placed at both ends of the dish.

English, marked Allertons, Mk. 88, L. V., c. 1908

DEAKIN PEARL

made by Deakin

The pitcher shown is painted cobalt blue on the leaves and the basket. There are red flowers in the basket and a grass green strip is placed under it. The basket and tendrils in the design are overlaid with copper lustre.

English, impressed Deakin, E.V., c 1840

DELPH

made by Wood & Sons

This coupe shaped dish has a rim that is outlined with small lozenge designs. These alternate with crossed straight lines.

The center pattern consists of stylized flowers that are circular and long thin leaves on branches that are placed from the outer border into the central design. The central pattern is a stylized basket of flowers with a tall handle. This same motif can be seen at Winterthur Museum on a China Trade plate. This identical pattern was issued by J. Kent as "Brugge".

English, marked as above, L.V., c 1907

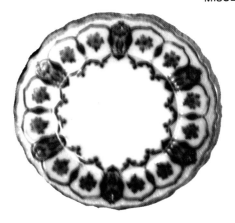

ECLIPSE

made by Johnson Bros.

This plate has a scalloped, gilded edge with floral and bead embossing. The border design consists of twelve oval reserves containing a flower, and six others that are webbed and contain a stylized design. This design enters the well and forms a circle of arches.

The well also is defined by fleur-de-lis embossing on the bottom part of the rim. The upper part of the design is gilded and so are the flowers.

English, marked as above, Mk. 2177, L.V., c 1891

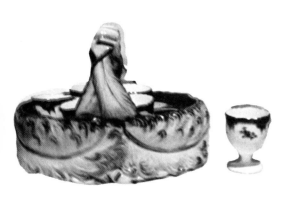

EGG BASKET

Maker unknown

The basket shown is decorated with heavy embossing in swirls. This is over-colored in blue and gold.

The center is molded with little openings to hold the egg cups as shown.

English, no markings, L.V., c 1895

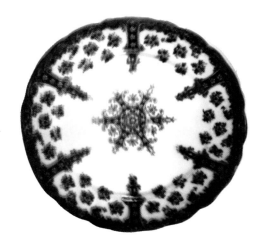

ELSA

made by W. & E. Corn

The scalloped gilded edge on this plate and its outer border is a blue strip about 5/8 inch deep printed with small flowers. Strap-like designs divide the plate into six sections with the straps entering the well. The spaces around the border are filled with single small flowers.

The center design is a baroque snowflake.

English, marked ⟨W⟩, Mk. 1113, L.V., c 1891

176

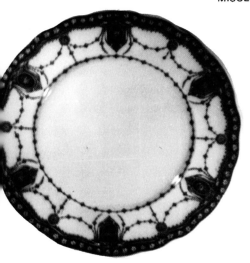

ETON

made by Till & Sons

This plate is printed in a grayish dark blue. It has unevenly scalloped edges that are outlined by a circle of small forget-me-not type flowers on a dark background. There is an embossing of small dots over this. The border is printed with shield-type medallions that enclose a rose. These are connected by chain garlands to form a circle.

The well is outlined by a necklace of beads.

English, marked as above, Mk. 3858, L.V., c 1880

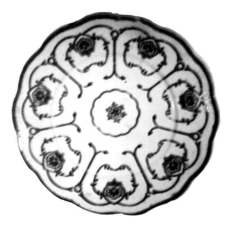

EXCELSIOR

made by Petrus Regout

This plate has a scalloped edge that is outlined with a narrow blue dotted line, embossing next encircles the rim. The design consists of abstract inverted hearts containing a shell enclosed in a leaf-shaped design to form a cartouche. These in turn are enclosed by curved lines that enter the well.

The center has a stylized flower set in a scalloped circle. This pattern may be borderline.

Dutch, marked as above with a sphinx mark, L. V., c 1900

FEATHER EDGE

made by Clementson & Young

This little dish has a dark blue border that has flow quality, and feathers toward the center. The body is soft and the color is creamy white. This is not a transfer pattern but was applied with a brush. As such, it is not Flow Blue but is of importance to Flow Blue understanding.

English, impressed marked as above, Mk. 911, E.V., c 1846

FISH PLATE

made by Wedgwood & Co.

The border is printed with three reserves with differing fish scenes in each. Alternating with these are scallop shells surrounded by large leaves and water lilies.

The central scene is of one large fish swimming through various seaweeds.

English, marked as above, Mk. 4059, L.V., c 1906

FLEUR-DE—LIS

made by J. & G. Meakin

There is a scalloped, gilded edge on this plate, and a dark blue banding with a tooth-like design pointing towards the center. Fleur-de-lis designs are placed around the rim over a net of small dots that terminate in points toward the well, creating a picket effect.

English, marked as above, Mk. 2601, L.V., c 1891

FLORAL

made by Thomas Hughes & Son

This tray has an unevenly scalloped edge outlined in gold. The rim is fluted by embossing and there are some scrolls embossed between the flutings. The outer rim is decorated with a narrow border of straight vertical lines. The rest of the rim is printed with chrysanthemums with dark leaves and foliated scrolls.

The center design is a fairly stylized circular pattern composed of small chrysanthemums with dark leaves and scrolls. This exact pattern was made in the United States, see "Royal Blue."

English, marked as above, Mk. 2122, L.V., c 1895

FLORENCE

made by Wood & Son

This plate is printed in grayish blue and with scroll and fleur-de-lis embossing and also a double line of embossing. The border is printed with small tea roses that have stems.

The well is defined by a ring of lace-like circles on the upper rim of the plate, and a gold circular line and inner border of little leaf sprigs. The well is then circled with a design of dotted wave-like linked scrolls and a narrow gold ring again circles the center of the well.

English, Registered 348701, marked as above, Mk. 4285, L.V., c 1900

GAME BIRDS

made by Copeland

These plates are deeply scalloped and heavily embossed with corrugated ridges that give a gadroon effect. The rim is sunken and rises to the edge of the well. The border is printed with three or more different designs; one of swirling feathers that form circles, one with lotus blossoms and arabesques, and another with a paisley-like design. All border prints extend into the well.

Each center design is of a different gamebird.

Reg. 180288, English, marked as above, Mk. 1076, L.V., c 1894

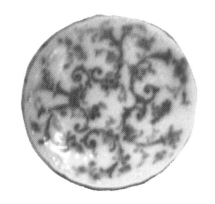

GAINSBOROUGH

made by Ridgways

This is a paisley type of overall decoration that is placed on a scalloped plate with an embossed edge.

English, marked as above, Mk. 3312, L.V., c 1905

GEM

made by Henry Alcock

The border pattern is a chain design that is enclosed in bands, and gilt is used to outline the top and the bottom of the band. Small beaded garlands depend from this band and swag into the well.

English, marked as above, Mk. 66, L.V., c 1891

GEM

made by John Meir & Son

The tureen pictured is printed in slate blue and it is scalloped and has a gilt edge. The pattern is of Japanese origin and is diapered on a slanting line across the top. The rest of the pattern consists of realistic peach blossoms on a bough and straight stemmed iris-like flowers.

English, marked J.M. & S., Mk. 2633, L.V., c 1891

GLENWOOD

made by Johnson Bros.

There is slate-blue printing on this unevenly scalloped plate. The edge is also enhanced with ½ inch scroll and floral embossing. The border is printed with ribbon bows and garlands of roses.

The well is outlined by a circle of little stylized flowers and a picket design composed of dots.

English, marked as above, Mk. 2177, L.V., c 1900

HANNIBAL

made by the Societe Ceramique

This plate has diaper circles around the edge. Four vignettes containing pictures of elephants are placed around the rim and alternate with floral patterns.

The center scene depicts Hannibal crossing the Alps with his foot soldiers, horsemen, and elephants.

Dutch, marked as above, made in Holland, L.V., c 1891

HAT PIN HOLDER

Maker unknown

This is part of a dresser set consisting of a perfume tray, pin tray, two covered boxes, and a ring tree. It is covered entirely with a very dark blue but space was left for printing of a lighter blue rose and some leaves at the base. Gold is heavily overpainted on all of this design.

English, L.V., c 1900

HEATH'S FLOWER

made by T. Heath

This platter has no name, and other pieces with this pattern that have been observed are unnamed also. For the sake of indexing and until the correct name is discovered, we will use the name given above.

The design that wreathes the border is applied heavily and in simple lines of flowers and leaves.

The center design is a grouping of the leaves around the central large five petalled flower.

This design is not a transfer print, it has been painted by hand.

English, impressed as above, Mk. 1995, E.V., c 1830

HOFBURG (THE)

made by W. H. Grindley

The bowl photographed has a gold line around the top that is unevenly scalloped. A blue line is set below this and follows the scalloped gold line. Below both is a design of a double scroll and dark oak leaves set around a greyish-blue orb.

English, marked as above, Mk. 1842, L.V. c 1891

HOLLAND

made by Johnson Bros.

This scalloped plate has an edge of tiny scallop embossing that is further detailed with a narrow blue line. The border is printed with blue onion forms and small stylized sprigs.

The well is encircled by a ring of stylized leaves. The center design is a bouquet of stylized oriental lotus, and lily and dahlia leaves, and a tree trunk.

English, marked as above, Mk. 2886, L.V., c 1891

HOLLAND (THE)

made by Alfred Meakin

The bowl shown is scalloped and has an embossed and gilded edge. The design on the border consists of six oval forms composed of stylized small flowers and stems, these alternate with a pendant design.

The center is detailed with a wreath of the same flowers that surround a snowflake that contains a central dot.

English, marked as above, Mk. 2586, L.V., c 1891

HOT WATER DISH

Maker unknown

The plate pictured has been affixed to a pewter well that has a spout and cap on it and handles affixed at each side. Hot water can be poured into the spout and food kept hot. The flown pattern is a tracing of seaweed. It is impossible to get to the backstamp in order to ascertain the pattern name or maker.

English, L.V., c 1890

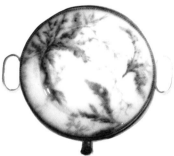

HUDSON

Made by S. Hancock & Son

This is a souvenir plate. For further information look under "Saratoga" made by the same firm. See page 199 this book.

English, marked R. & M., L.V., c 1905

IDA

made by Brownfields

The surface of a footed compote is shown. Its edge is gently scalloped and defined with a lacy trim. The border has three large reserves that contain a picture of castle-like towers and three smaller wreathed medallions that enclose a drawing of two urns. The entire background for these is covered with a soft blue and darker blue flowers. The border terminates in scrolls and garlands that encircle the well.

English, marked as above, Mk. 670, L.V., c 1891

ILFORD

made by Ford & Sons Ltd.

The top of a small sauce tureen is shown. This is printed in a greyish blue and the top is outlined with a Greek key design. The border is printed in six oblong reserves separated by vertical bands containing a stylized heart and flower motif. The reserves are filled with a fish scale diaper design and each is centered with a floral medallion.

English, marked as above, Mk. 1585, L.V., c 1908

INDIANA

made by Wedgwood & Co.

The outer rim of this plate is detailed by a ring of little squares in each of which there is a small design. The border is printed with stylized round flowers and thin long leaves. The design enters halfway into the well.

English, marked as above, Mk. 4055, M.V., c 1870

184

IVANHOE

made by Wedgwood

This plate is one of a set of dinner dishes. The plates depict different events in the romance novel "Ivanhoe" by Sir Walter Scott. The border is a pattern of pairs of fowls, fish, and rabbits. Six medallions are set on this background and contain the faces of "Richard the Lion Hearted," "Rowena," "Rebecca," "Isaac of York," "The Templar," and "Wamba."

The center scene on this plate reads "Urfried relating her story to Cedric." "Knight Templar" is offered as a pattern by Wedgwood, but this is another name for one of the plates in this set.

English, marked as above, Mk. 4088, L.V., c 1901

IVY

Maker unknown

The pitcher shown was sold as "Ivy." It has no name plate transfer on the bottom, so this name will do until someone discovers the correct title.

The top is deeply scalloped and there is scalloped embossing. The top and the base collars are of dark blue. The body of the pitcher is of a pale blue. A design of ivy is printed on the body of the pitcher and overlaid in place with very dark blackish blue. Gold is used to outline the veins in the leaves.

Probably English, L.V., c 1880

185

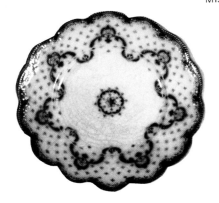

KEELE

made by W. H. Grindley

This plate has a scalloped, beaded, and gilded edge and also a line of scroll embossing that is set upon the upper rim which is printed in dark blue. The rest of the rim is printed with fleur-de-lis.. Over this background there is a design of scrolls that form arches. In the top of each arch there is a single small flower and a large pendant fleur-de-lis. The arches are joined at the bottom by small scrolls that form an arc, each set with a leafy-shaped fleur-de-lis.

The center design is a scalloped circle that encloses a snowflake design which is also decorated with fleur-de-lis.

English, marked as above, Mk. 1842, L.V., c 1891

KENWORTH

made by Johnson Bros.

This is a twelve sided plate that has a lightly paneled rim which is outlined with a simple blue edge. A large pattern of blackberries and leaves is placed on one side of the plate and the leaves, berries, and tendrils trail into the center. This pattern was also printed on a deeply scalloped plate with much embossing by the same maker. "Blackberry" is another name for "Kenworth."

English, marked as above, Mk. 2179, L.V., c 1900

LA BELLE LOVELY LADIES

made by Wheeling Potteries

This plate has an unevenly and deeply scalloped edge detailed with gilt and scroll and shell embossing. The border is printed in very deep cobalt blue. There is an embossing of flowers on the border that is touched with white. Gold flowers are traced around the outer rim also.

The well is defined with shell embossing on a gold circle. The center scene is of two women in a field near a flowering tree. They are dressed in Greek classical fashion. "La Belle" Flow Blue pieces also come in a coloured scene with animals, such as rabbits, and also with pictures of large full blown roses. All of these are in multi-color.

American, marked Wheeling Potteries (see Thorn p. 154), Mk. 28, L.V., c 1891

LA FRANCAIS

made by the French China Co.

This platter has a scalloped gilded edge and is deeply embossed with scrolls and fleur-de-lis. The upper border is printed in deep blue that fades toward the center. There are small gold lace-like medallions overprinted on the rim. The well is defined by a thin gold band.

The center scene on this platter is a small Dutch scene with windmill, houses, and a sailing boat.

American, marked "La Francais" made by the French China Co. (Thorn p. 126), Mk. 24, L.V., c 1890

LOIS

made by The New Wharf Pottery

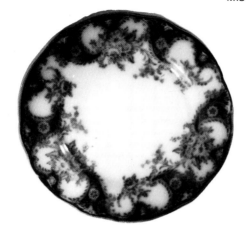

This plate has a scalloped rim with a very dark blue edging. There is shell and scallop embossing around the rim. The border design is composed of six feather-like swirls each enclosing a little star. In the spaces provided by the swirls bouquets of mixed flowers alternate with a single full blown rose with stem and leaves. The entire border design enters the well.

English, marked as above, Mk. 2886, L.V., c 1891

LONSDALE

made by Ridgways

This deeply scalloped plate has an embossed edge, which gives a gadroon effect, and is typical of Ridgways. The border is printed with grapes and grape leaves and tendrils. Some of these extend into and cross the well. The example pictured has gold decorations on the veins of the leaves, but not all "Lonsdale" has gold trim.

English, marked as above, Mk. 3313, L.V., c 1910

LOUVRE

made by J. & G. Meakin

There is a greyish-blue printing on this plate. It has an unevenly scalloped edge with feather embossing and some gilt on the embossing. The border is printed with baroque medallions that alternate with small bouquets of flowers in a basket-like design. The bottom of the rim pattern forms a circle around the well.

English, marked as above, Mk. 2600, L.V., c 1890

LUNÉVILLE

made by Keller & Guerin

This is a pale blue printed plate that has a tulip-like pattern around the rim that alternates with a fleur-de-lis type design.

The center of the well is almost covered with a formal grouping of these two designs connected in the center with a pattern of small dots.

French, marked K. & G. Opaque Granite, Thorn p. 87, Mk. 3 L.V., c 1891

LUNÉVILLE BLUE

made by Keller & Guerin

This plate has an unevenly scalloped edge with leafy scrolls set around the edge at six places. The entire rim is covered with a deep flowing blue, this enters the well and fades out toward the center.

The center is specked with blue dots and so is the reverse side of this plate.

French, marked K. & G., Opaque Granite, Thorn p. 87, Mk. 3, L.V., c 1891

LUNÉVILLE ONION

made by Keller & Guerin

The plate pictured is printed in a soft dark greyish blue. The border is printed with the traditional stylized onions, flowers, and sprigs. The central design is of stylized oriental flowers, leaves, and a tree trunk.

French, marked as above, Cushion & Honey p. 75, L.V., c 1891

MADISON

made by J. & G. Meakin

This pattern is printed in greyish-blue. The edge of the plate shown is outlined with two narrow gold bands separated by a row of little straight lines. The border is printed with oval medallions, leafy scrolls, and wreaths set over a pin-point dotted blue background. The well is circled by a ring like that on the outer edge.

The center design is of a pair of sprays of ivy leaves set on two sides of the well.

English, marked as above, Mk. 2603, L.V., c 1910

MARLBOROUGH

made by W. H. Grindley

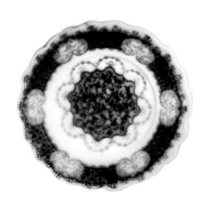

The scalloped beaded edge of this plate is detailed with floral embossing. The border is printed with six scrolled cartouche forms that enclose a stylized bell flower. These are joined by a honeycomb diaper pattern. The well is outlined by a row of small scalloped embossing.

The center design is a scalloped eight sided rounded figure covered with a paisley design on a dotted field. This is surrounded by garlands of bell flowers, with a small flower placed in each enclosure.

English, marked as above, Mk. 1842, L.V., c 1891

MARQUIS, THE

made by W. H. Grindley

The plate photographed is unevenly scalloped and is embossed around the edge with a thick ridge that follows the scallops and which has fleur-de-lis at eight evenly spaced points; this ridge is heavily gilded. The border is covered with very dark blue and terminates at the well with a fleur-de-lis edging that gives a picket effect around the well.

The center design is a large blue circle outlined with fleur-de-lis. Small slender gold flowers are overprinted on each of the projections formed by the fleur-de-lis, and a gold, lacy medallion is overprinted in the center.

English, marked as above, Mk. 1843, #4733130, L.V. c 1906

MARTHA WASHINGTON

Maker unknown

This pattern is a copy of that on a tea set a Dutch merchant, "Van Braan Houchgest," who had been many times in China, presented to Mrs. Washington in 1796. The design is symbolistic. Her initials in the center are surrounded by the rays of "The rising sun of the Republic." This is surrounded by a wreath and a ribbon with a motto that translates "Honor and Defense Come From It." On the rim is a chain, each link contains the name of a state, fifteen links in all, including Kentucky that had just come in as a state. On the outer edge is a circle that is made up of a snake biting its tail, an old symbol of eternity and continuity.

English, marked "Made in England," L.V., c 1900

MEISSEN

made by Ridgways

This saucer has a scalloped edge and a narrow blue band encircles it about ½ inch from the edge.

The design covers the plate and consists of typical stylized flowers, leaves, and stems and tree trunk.

The plate has a backstamp of a crown and a circle and is labeled Meissen and England.

English, could be Mk. 3312, L.V., c 1910

MILAN

made by W. H. Grindley

This plate has an unevenly scalloped edge and a fine picket design outlines its rim. The border is printed with three baroque pendant designs that terminate in little leafy garlands that enter the well. These alternate with shorter versions of the same pattern. Garlands of flowers and leaves link the two elements of the design.

English, marked as above, Mk. 1842, Reg. 213153, L.V., c 1893

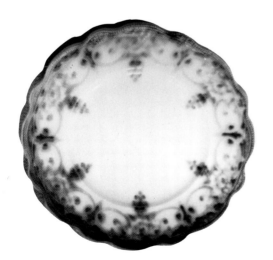

MONARCH

made by Myott Son & Co.

This deeply scalloped plate has a beaded, embossed, and gilded edge. The border has a design of a large peony-like flower joined by long reverse "C" curves and a stylized fleur-de-lis design. Extending from the bottom of each flower group is a pendant design that enters the well. The well is defined by a row of tiny embossed dots on the rim.

English, marked as above, Mk. 2811, L.V., c 1907

MONGOLIA

made by Johson Bros.

The border on this plate is printed with a field of interlaced loops, some are printed darker than the others, and these form circular bands. Four medallions are set into the border and contain small bouquets. The well is defined by a circle of double lines.

The center scene is of two long-legged birds with trailing curved tail feathers.

English, marked as above, Mk. 2177, L.V., c 1900

MORRISAN

made by Doulton

The pitcher shown has a top border of roses with thin stems and leaves. The body is covered with a procession of women and children who are dancing under a grape arbor. "Morris" is an old English verb meaning "to dance."

English, marked as above, Mk. 1329, L.V., c 1891

MOYUNE

made by Ridgways

The border of this plate resembles oriental lambrequins. It is divided into six sections by arch forms, and these form a six sided center section. Flowers of the border enter the well. In three arches are scrolled fleur-de-lis, and in the other three arches are peonies.

The center design is of wide open peony-like flowers with dark leaves. At the bottom of these flowers is a small table-like pedestal.

English, marked as above, Mk. 3312, L.V., c 1905

NANKIN

made by Ashworth

The rim of this plate is outlined with a Gothic type border of bell-like forms. The border is printed with an oriental design of flowers and a little jar that is set on a railing.

The center design is of a wide footed basin filled with peonies and dahlias and prunus. This is supported by a geometric band design, and at the far right there is a little covered urn with tall, long handles.

English, marked Ironstone, Ashworth, Mk. 137, M.V., c 1865

NORMANDY

made by Johnson Bros.

The plate photographed has a gently scalloped and gilded edge with a blue printed band and ruffled embossing. A lightly printed row of tiny flowers encircles the plate inside the embossing. The border is printed with very heavy blue ivy-type leaves, the veins of which are detailed in gold. The stems of the leaves enter the well. The tiny flower border is repeated around the well.

English, marked as above, Mk. 2177, L.V., c 1900

PAISLEY

made by Mercer

These plates have scalloped gilded edges with scrolled embossing around the rim. An all over design of asters and baroque scrolls cover the plate and gives the pattern for which this is named. No name is on the backstamp, therefore, this name will be used until the correct name is discovered.

American, marked as above, (see Hartman), Mk. 19 L.V., c 1890

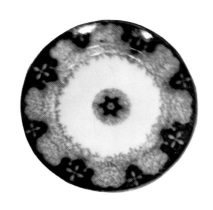

PERSIAN MOSS

made by Utzschneider & Co.

This gilt edged plate has a dark blue border which is applied in rounded triangular forms at eight points. Inset at each of these is a quatrefoil. All of this is overlaid on a web-work of small rounded cloud-like lines that extend into the well.

The center medallion shows a snowflake form surrounded by the same little mossy lines. There are gold outlines on the border detail and on the center snowflake.

German, marked Sarreguemines, Mk. 6, (p. 74 Hartman), L.V., c 1891

PERUVIAN HORSE HUNT

made by Anthony Shaw

These are vivid blue equestrian scenes on this plate. The border is composed of reserves depicting a rider and two horses. These are joined by a small belt-like cartouche containing a little bouquet of roses.

The center scene shows a group of wild horses leaping over a waterfall in a chasm as their pursuers rein up. There is mountain scenery in the background. The backstamp contains two rearing stallions. The Staffordshire Potteries made china for export to South America as well as to the United States. The example shown does not flow, but is sold as Flow Blue, and may come in Flow Blue.

English, marked as above, Mk. 3497, M.V., (the plate is dated January 8, 1853)

PHEASANT

made by Francis Morley

This plate has sixteen narrow panels and its rim has a pattern of flower sprays and cartouches that contain a diaper pattern.

The center scene shows a large pheasant at left that is sitting on a branch of a flowering lotus tree. A large insect flies above the flowers at upper right.

A saucer in this same pattern is marked F. M. & Co. with identical backstamp. This plate, as a matter of fact, is marked R. & M. This mark would be 3278, and is for Ridgway, Morley which became F. M. & Co. in 1844. The mark on the saucer stands for Francis Morley, although it is thought that Ridgway made the pattern first.

English, "Stoneware F. M. & Co.", Mk. 3278, E.V., c 1845

PICKWICK "DICKENS"

made by Ridgway

Ridgway's gadroon border appears on this scalloped plate. The border is completely printed with full rose blooms, leaves, and buds. This border design enters the well for ¾ inch.

The center scene is outlined by an acorn shaped design that gives a beading effect. The center scenes in this set of dishes depict various illustrations by Seymour and Phiz, the original illustrators of the "Pickwick Papers."

English, Reg. 419412, marked as above, L.V., c 1904

POMONA

made by Frank Beardmore & Co.

The gravy boat shown is printed in a slate blue. It has a border design of small trailing garlands on a dark background that is outlined with scrolls. The designs of piles of fruit alternate with cartouched lattice forms that also contain fruit.

Pomona was the Roman Goddess of fruit trees.

English, marked F. B. & Co. Ltd., Mk. 307, Reg. 576811, L.V., c 1909

REBECCA

made by George Jones

This plate had no name, so it is herein called for the lady who brought it to be photographed. The border is printed with a balustered effect. The well is covered with a circular design of three-leaf clovers looped together. The center circle has a snowflake trimming.

English, marked G. J. & Sons, Mk. 2218, L.V., c 1900

RICHMOND

made by Burgess & Leigh

The egg cup shown is printed in a fairly light blue. The design consists of swirls of scrolls. In the scrolls are flower filled spaces. The swirls form reserves in which are placed two flowers and their stems. The upper border is composed of a miniature paisley design.

English, marked B. & L., Mk. 712, Reg. 438212, L.V., c 1904

RICHMOND

made by Ford & Sons

This plate has a scalloped gilded edge. Its border is printed with nasturtiums and leaves set in triangular reserves. These are connected around the top of the border by a design of small stylized flowers. At the bottom are oblong designs that contain scrolls which have pendant patterns coming from them that enter the well.

The center design is of a medallion with an open center.

English, marked as above, Mk. 1585, L.V., c 1900

ROYAL BLUE

made by Burgess & Campbell

The scalloped edge of this plate is outlined by gilt, which is also applied in little scallops. The border is printed with chrysanthemums with stylized leaves and stems.

The center design is of two flowers and the stylized stems are placed to form a circular pattern. There is a heavy navy lustre over the leaves, and the veins of the leaves are gilded.

This same pattern was made in England, see Floral by Hughes.

American, made by Burgess & Campbell, (see Thorn p. 120), Mk. 33, L.V., c 1880

SARATOGA

made by S. Hancock & Son

This is a souvenir plate issued by the famous firm that made souvenir plates for American resorts and cities.

Depicted is the town of Saratoga in upstate New York. Another plate called "Hudson" by the same maker is pictured in this book.

The mark "Rowland & Marcellus" that appears on the backstamp stood for china importers in New York City. Thousands of these historical scenic views were imported from 1898 to 1900.

English, marked Rowland & Marcellus Co., L. V., c 1900

SAXON

made by Clementson Bros.

This plate has a scalloped edge with criss-cross embossing. The border is printed with swirling forms that contain a columbine-type flower and its buds. The well is defined by a ring of oriental design.

The center pattern is of a star surrounded by the same flower patterns that appear on the border.

English, marked as above, Mk. 909, L.V., c 1910

SHELL

made by E. Challinor

The edge of this plate is outlined by a diapered ¾ inch deep border. The rim is printed with three pointed arabesque designs with scrolls that alternate with three groups of blossoms, buds and leaves.

The center design is of a conch shell laying on its side and a cowrie shell upright next to it. Overscaled flowers and sprigs surround these shells.

English, marked E. C., Mk. 835, M.V., c 1860

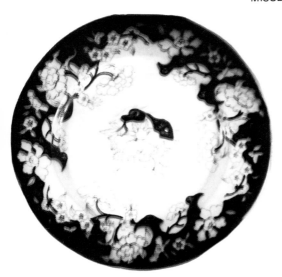

SMYRNA

made by Ridgway & Abington

The edge of this plate is gently scalloped with six very long curves. Its border is printed in a blackish blue. Peonies and sprays of blossoms are printed lightly against this dark border. The blossoms and leaves enter the well.

The center design is of ruffled peonies, some daisy-like flowers, and very dark heavy leaves.

The backstamp on this plate appears in Jervis (China Classics 3), p. 103, plate 3, mark 8.

English, E.V., c 1840

SPHINX

made by Charles Meigh

There is a gently scalloped edge on this plate. The handles of the hot plate shown are embossed scrolls. The border is printed with pairs of winged sphinx figures that face each other on either side of a stork. Alternating with these is a pair of wings. The well is defined by a circle of stylized papyrus bunches.

In the center of the plate is a winged sphinx, which is set in a circle design.

English, impressed C. M., Mk. 2614, E.V., c 1840

SPINACH

made by Libertas

This pattern is also known as "Turkey Feather" and "Oatmeal." It was given as a premium with cereal in this country (United States). It is a simple primitive design of a wreath made of long leaves and centered with a large sprig of the same leaves. The insides of bowls and cups are bordered with a feather design, and in the inside of the bowls there is a medallion composed of triple circles surrounded by pointed wide leaves.

Prussian, marked as above, L.V., c 1900

STANLEY

made by Johnson Bros.

This plate has an unevenly scalloped edge that is outlined by comb tooth embossing. The border is printed with six stylized lotus blossoms with two little pendant bell flowers. These alternate with six double scroll forms from which emerge a pair of stylized daisies.

English, marked as above, Mk. 2177, L.V., dated November 7, 1898

STELLA

made by Bovey

Grey-blue printing is used on this tureen. It is decorated in empire style with darkened panels of straight vertical lines, gold scrolls, fleur-de-lis, and garlands of small gold dotted flowers.

English, marked as above, Mk. 2981, L.V., c 1905

STERLING

made by Colonial Stirling Co.

This creamer has a blue border outlined in gold at the top of its collar. Gold lacy medallions are printed on the blue edging. It is backstamped "Sterling U.S.A."

American, marked as above. Patented 1918.

STRAWBERRY

probably made by T. Walker

This is a twelve sided plate but it is not paneled. It has a blue line around the edge. The border and plate well are printed with dark, large blue leaves, and strawberries are placed in the well. This plate could be dated from the stilt marks to about 1856. Laidacker states that a pattern called "Strawberry" was made by T. Walker in 1856, and he pictures it on page 84 in Volume 1. It is very like this example.

English, E.V. to M.V., c 1856

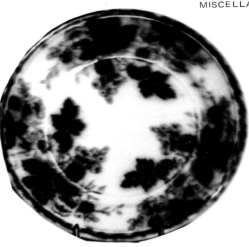

STRAWBERRY LUSTER

made by Mellor Venables

This plate has eight panels and its edge is outlined with a running curving line. The border is printed with three large groups of strawberries and leaves. These enter the well. The leaves are decorated with dark gold luster.

See Laidacker, Vol. 1, p. 85, M.V., c 1865

SUTHERLAND BORDER

made by Charles Meigh & Son

This plate has a scalloped gilded edge and a ½ inch border of lines and dots outlines the rim. The border is printed with large scrolls, poppies, and tassels. These are heavily gilded. The design enters the well to form a complete circle.

The center flower is one large stemmed bloom, and a bud with very small serrated leaves.

English, marked C. M. & S., like Mk. 2620, M.V., c 1855

(Reissued later by Royal Doulton, named Sutherland, c. 1905+)

TILE

Maker unknown

This is one of four tiles that illustrate the seasons of the year. It says "Sunlight and Flowers." The girl is dressed in Victorian garb and holds a fan.

Engiish, M.V., c 1870

TRENT

made by Ford & Son

This bowl has a scalloped edge and its border is printed with daisy-like flowers and a diaper pattern of small dotted squares. The well is outlined by beading. The border design is composed of wild roses and leaves in pattern groups alternating with pendant small flowers. These are connected with bead garland.

The center design is a bouquet of small stemmed flowers.

English, marked as above, Mk. 1585, L.V., c 1900

TRENT I

made by Wood & Son

This plate has a border that is printed in deep cobalt. Upon close inspection, it is noted that it is printed in vertical slanting lines. Lacy gold half wreaths are overprinted on the rim.

The center design is a picture of three women in Grecian costumes who are standing on a terrace.

English, marked as above, Mk. 4285, L.V., c 1891

VERONA

made by Ridgways

This plate has a scalloped rim that is outlined in very dark blue. There is linear and dotted and curved embossing around its edge. The border is printed in Ridgway's rich grey-blue with reserves left open for small flowers. Five little bouquets of daisies and a wild rose are placed around the rim. Swags of daisy chains enter the well. Gold has been used heavily around the edge and around the scroll design that outlines the well.

English, marked as above, Mk. 3313, L.V., c 1910

VERONA

made by Wood & Son

The gently scalloped gilt edge of this plate has a border of embossing. The plate is multicolored with a greyish-green used on the scrolls and leaves and on some of the flower designs. The border is printed with four large pink peonies alternating with red poppies. Deep cobalt blue is used in the background.

The center scene is set off by a ring of blue, gold, and green flowers. The entire well is covered by a design of two large peonies, a large poppy, and many green tendrils, and cobalt blue leaves.

English, marked as above, Mk. 4285, L.V., c 1891

VINE

made by Davenport

This platter has a gently scalloped, gilt outlined edge. A border of large grape leaves and vines circle the well, the veins of the leaves and the stems are outlined in gold.

The center shows one large grape leaf surrounded by several smaller ones.

English, marked Davenport Longport, Mk. 1189, L.V., Dated April 1883

VINRANKA, PERCY

made by (Cefle) Upsala Ekeby

This plate is unevenly scalloped and is embossed with short vertical ribbing. The border is covered with a design of large vine leaves on stems, and groups of small berries. These, with the addition of trailing small leaves, form a wreath around the rim.

Swedish, marked U.E. (Upsala-Ekeby) "Vinranka" Percy.

Modern, c 1968

VIRGINIA

made by John Maddock & Sons

The scalloped embossed edge of this plate is gilt outlined. The pattern is asymetrical with grape leaves and tendrils placed to one side in a mass with tendrils extending across the plate at the top and the bottom. The veins of the leaves are detailed in gold.

English, marked as above, Mk. 2463, L.V., c 1891

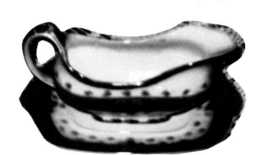

WEIR

made by Ford & Sons

The gravy boat and tray in this picture have scalloped gilt edges. A dark blue border is printed around the rim and this has light blue flowers in it. Where flowers are printed on the border there are spear-like points. A row of small floral dots encircles the plate above the well.

English, marked F. & Sons, Mk. 1585, L.V., c 1900

WINDSOR SCROLL

could be Thomas Dimmock Jr.

This plate is scalloped and its rim is printed with thick scrolls, and with three stylized bell flowers and three roses that alternate with each other. There is a gold painted circle set inside the well and the center design is a pin wheel composed of short thick scrolls.

English, marked with a monogram, could be, Mk. 1300, E.V., c 1845

No Picture Available

AULD LANG SYNE

Maker unknown

A cup observed in a catalogue was over-sized (a farmers cup), and was decorated with bucolic country scenes. Inside the rim is part of the verse that gives the pattern its name: "We'll take a cup of kindness yet"

English, L.V., c 1900

BLACKBERRY

This is the familiar name for "Kenworth" by Johnson Bros.

BLUE MEISSEN

This is another popular name for Holland by Johnson Bros. Holland is the correct name. It is also called the Onion pattern.

BRUGGE

made by J. Kent

This is exactly the same as "Delph" by Wood & Sons.

Reg. #S43416, Mk. 2266, L.V., c 1910

CHAIN OF STATES

This is another name for "Martha Washington."

DENMARK

made by Furnivals

A plate observed with this name has a meissen-type design all over the surface This is composed of simple pattern lines.

English, marked as above, Mk. 1652, L.V., c 1905

DENMARK

made by Minton

This platter was displayed in a catalogue. It is eight sided and its border is covered with a design that includes triangular art mouveau designs at the eight corners. These are linked by a design of stylized round flowers flanked by slender leaves. The well is defined by a ring of cross hatching.

The center design is a circle composed of an outer ring of the stylized flowers and an inner circle of art motifs.

English, marked as above, L.V. 1900.

FLAMINGO

made by Ashworth Bros.

This scalloped edge plate has peach lustre on the rim. Pictures of flamingos are printed in the well.

English, marked as above, Mk. 147, L.V., c 1885

FORTUNA

made by J. & G. Meakin

This is a pattern of fruit and flowers.

English, Mk. 2602, L.V., c 1907

HAGUE

made by Johson Bros.

These plates have slightly and unevenly scalloped edges, enhanced by scroll embossing and also shell embossing that extends from the edge of the plate vertically to the well. The pattern consists of short stems of fern-like leaves and stylized flowers. The center design is of a long-stemmed stylized flower.

English, marked as above, Mk. 2177, L.V., c 1900

KNIGHT TEMPLAR

made by Wedgwood

According to a letter received from Josiah Wedgwood & Sons Ltd. no pattern was ever made with the above name although it is advertised by dealers. This is a part of the set of "Ivanhoe" made by Wedgwood.

MAPLE LEAF

made by New Wharf Pottery

Mk. 2886, L.V., c 1891

PERCY

made by Cefie

See Vinranka

ROOSEVELT

Maker unknown

A jardiniere observed in a sales catalogue has a dark blue body with embossing that is highlighted with gold. Reserves were left on the sides and in these appear a large cow and a calf.

English probably, L.V., c 1891.

RUBUS

made by Villeroy & Boch

This design is printed in a very dark, blackish blue. The word Rubus, in Latin, means bramble bush or blackberry bush, and the pattern is exactly that. It shows black-berries, bramble branches and leaves.

German, marked as above with "Mett-lach" see Thorne pg. 37, Mk. 40, L.V., c 1885

SEFTON

made by Ridgways

This plate has a scalloped edge that is outlined with scroll embossing. The outer border is printed in blue scrolls. The lower border has a pattern of garlands of forget-me-nots that have trailing ends toward the well. These are evenly spaced around the rim. The scalloped well is outlined by a circle of the same little flowers. There is some gold on this pattern.

English, marked as above, Mk. 3312, c 1905

STRATFORD

made by W. H. Grindley

This dinner set was made with octag-onally shaped pieces. The pattern consists of blossoms and very large plume-like scrolls that alternate around the rim and extend into the well. Gold was used to highlight the details and the plate edges. This is very much like "Argyle" by Grindley, and may be the same pattern.

English, marked as above, Mk. 1842, L. V., c 1891

VERONA

made by New Wharf Pottery

This is the same as "Verona" by Wood & Sons. New Wharf Pottery was taken over by Wood & Sons in 1894

English, marked as above, Mk. 2886, L.V., c 1891

Patterns Inadvertently
Omitted from Categories

FLORAL

OPHIR

made by E. Bourne and J.E. Leigh

This plate has a scalloped gilded edge with feather embossing and some scroll embossing. It has a baroque floral pattern around the outer rim. Small bouquets are scattered at six points on the border, and parts of these enter the well. These are connected with a point d'esprit effect. Gold is used on the scrolls and on some of the flowers.

Ophir is the name of the land mentioned in the Bible, Kings I, 10:11, from whence came gold and jewels and rare trees for King Solomon.

English, marked as above, (See Thorne, Pg. 48), Mk. 10, L.V., c. 1891

ORMONDE

made by Alfred Meakin

This plate has an unevenly scalloped edge that is trimmed with scrools and comb embossing. The border is printed in two shades of blue, one of which is very dark. The design is composed of scrools, lily-of-the-valley, and dahlia-like flowers.

The center design is a small bouquet of a pair of single petaled dahlias and sprigs.

English, marked as above, Mk. 2586, L.V. c. 1891

PARIS

made by Al. Fred Colley & Co. Ltd.

This plate is embossed around the edge with two bands of fleur-de-lis set over pale blue, and outlined by a darker edging.

The pattern is predominantly on the rim and consists of three large groups of poppies, leaves, and swirling stems. These enter the well.

English, marked as above, Mk. 999, L.V. c 1909

WALL PLAQUES
11½" H., 10½" W., 1½" D.

GAME DISH (RABBITS)

*made by W. T. Copeland & Sons
(Dated 1904).*

ROME

made by Sampson Bridgwood

DEVON

Made by Brownfields Guild Pottery Society

Cheese dish, consisting of tray and wedge shaped cover, decorated with sprays of daisies.

English, marked BGP, Mk. 668, c. 1900.

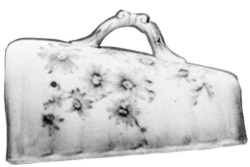

PHOENIX BIRDS

Maker Unknown

There is no mark on this dish. This name used to catalogue the pattern. Probably c. 1850.

BASKET JAPAN

maker unknown

The rim design on this plate consists of floral reserves that hold a peony and some sprigs. These reserves alternate with spaces filled at the top of the rim with an oval diaper and at the bottom with pairs of dahlias. Both designs cover the cavetto and form a wreath. In the center of the well an exotic bird perches upon a rock form at left. The basket of the title is in the right foreground and is filled with flowers. At the extreme right a tall flowering tree rises and bend over the top center.

SMITH'S JAPAN

made by Minton

The dark upper part of the concave rim of this plate is decorated with four triangular scrolled reserves that contain a five petalled flower. The triangles are representations of the handles used on short Japanese swords. In the arches formed by the dark areas the rim is covered with pairs of large flowers that resemble peonies. In the center an overscaled exotic flower surrounded by bamboo, leaves, fronds and buds, rises from a base compounded on large rock forms and part of a trellis fence.

The rim and reverse side of this plate are pale blue where the cobalt used in the underprinting has caused a flow blue quality, but the pattern is borderline Flow Blue.

English, marked B.B. (Imp.) and New Stone (Imp.) and M&Co. ptd. like Gk2692, dated 1852

214

A Note on the Word "Japan"

When Japan is used in a pattern name it denotes a decorative method in which cobalt blue was used for the transfer printing of an oriental subject. After the dish was glazed, bright enamel colours, predominately dark red (rouge-de-fer), sometimes green and a few other strong colours, plus gilt, were applied to the pattern details. The oriental subjects ranged from the flower basket pattern, a wicker basket with high handles which contains a bouquet conventialized chrysanthemums (sometimes contained in a circle), pine and bamboo branches, rock forms and fence sections, to small tables holding flower pots. These designs became popular in the early 1800s as they were relatively inexpensive and very colourful.

* * * * * * * * * * * * * * * * *

CARMANIA

Made by Wood & Son

This pattern is identical to Touraine made by Alcock and by Stanley. English marked as above Mk. 4285, c. 1900.

BRUSH STROKE
maker unknown

BIBLIOGRAPHY

Antique Glass and China. Geoffrey A. Godden. 1966

Encyclopedia of British Pottery and Porcelain Marks. Geoffrey A. Godden. 1964

Staffordshire Pottery. Wedgwood and Ormsbee. 1947

Early American Pottery and China. John Spargo. Reprint 1948

British Pottery and Porcelain. Geoffrey A. Godden. 1963

Marks and Monograms on European and Oriental Pottery and Porcelain. W. Chaffers. 14th Revised Edition.

Staffordshire Pottery and Its History. Josiah Wedgewood. 1912

Chinnery & China Coast Painting. Berry-Hill. 1970

History of the Staffordshire Potteries. Simeon Shaw. (1829) Reprint 1968

Porcelain and Pottery Marks. Harman. 1943

English China and its Marks. Ormsbee. 1959

Dictionary of Marks — Pottery and Porcelain. Ralph M. and Terry H. Kovel. 14th Printing, 1968

*Anglo-American China. Part 1 and Part 2. Sam Laidacker. 1954

William Adams, an Old English Potter. Turner. 1904

An Illustrated Encyclopedia of British Pottery & Porcelain. Godden.

The Blue-China Book. Ada Camehl. 1916 Reprinted 1946

* Old China. Minnie Watson Kamm. 3rd printing, 1970

Staffordshire Blue. W. L. Little. 1969

Handbook of Pottery and Porcelain Marks. Cushion and Honey.

Handbook of Old Pottery and Porcelain Marks. J. Jordan Thorn. 1947

The Earthenware Collector. G. Wooliscroft and Phead R. E. Arca.

English China Collecting for Amateurs. J. P. Cushion. 1967.

Hints on Household Taste. Charles L. Eastlake. 1868. Dover, 1969

Chinese Export Porcelain for the American Trade, 1785-1835. Jean McClure Mudge. 1962

Baroque Cartouches. Johann Krausse.

Victorian Pottery. Wakefield. 1962

Staffordshire Pottery. Josiah Wedgwood & Thomas Hamilton Ormsbee. 1947

The Country Life Pocket Book of China. G. Bernard Hughes. 1965

American Historical Views on Staffordshire China. Larsen. 1950

*China Classics 4. Ironstone. Larry Freeman. 1954

*China Classics 6. English Staffordshire. Serry Wood. 1959 (Kamm)

*China Classics 3. European China. W. P. Jervis. 1953 revised

You may enjoy perusing the above list of books. Those marked * are valuable to you in acquiring particular knowledge about flow blue transfer china.

GLOSSARY

ARABESQUE Surface decoration in colour composed in flowing lines of branches, leaves and scroll work fancifully intertwined.

BAROQUE Irregularly shaped, and/or extravagantly decorated.

CARTOUCHE An oval or oblong figure enclosing a design.

CROCKET A small ornament, usually a plant or leaf form, placed on steeply inclined surfaces, such as copings of roof gables, and which turns up from the surface and returns upon itself to form a knob-like termination; seen in Gothic and Victorian architecture.

DIAPER A linen fabric woven with small constantly repeated figures such as diamonds. Diaper Pattern — such geometrical or conventional pattern used to form the ground of a design.

DORMER A projecting vertical window in the sloping roof of a house.

EPI A finial, an ornament placed upon the apex of a roof.

FOLIATED Consisting of, or ornamented with leaves or leaf-work.

GAZEBO A summerhouse built on a site that affords an enjoyable view.

JUNK A large oriental sailboat with square prow and square sails, flat bottomed and with a high stern.

LAMBREQUIN In ceramics, ornamentation consisting of solid color with a jagged or scalloped edge, a curtain-like band.

MANDARIN A government official with one of nine ranks in the days of the Chinese Empire.

MAURESQUE (MORESQUE) Moorish in style or ornamental design.

MEDALLION An oval or circular panel in a decorative design.

PAGODA A temple or sacred building, especially sacred tower built over the remains of a saint.

PARAPET A low wall placed at the edge of a platform, or along the sides of a bridge to prevent people from falling over.

PRUNUS In oriental pottery a representation of the Chinese or Japanese species of Rosacex which contains plums, peaches, almonds, etc.

ROCOCO Having the characteristics of Louis XIV or Louis V workmanship such as shell-and scroll-work.

SAMPAN A small boat propelled by a single scull over the stern, and with a roof made of mats.

TREFOIL An ornamental figure representing a three leafed clover.

TREILLAGE Lattice work, a trellis.

INDEX OF PATTERNS

O – oriental   F – floral
S – scenic   AN – art nouveau
M – miscellaneous

Layout and Photographic Illustrations
for the text by
Marguerite R. Weber

TYPESETTING BY VARI-COMP INC.

PRINTING BY HAMILTON PRINTING

LOUISVILLE, KENTUCKY

FRONT PIECE AND STUDIO PHOTOGRAPHS

BOB KELLOGG